Nee-Nee,

Thank you so much for your support!

Always keep Smiling!

SHAKIN' NOT STIRRED

FINDING PERSEVERENCE THROUGH PARKINSON'S

BY
DAVID CHEDESTER

authorHOUSE®

AuthorHouse™
1663 Liberty Drive
Bloomington, IN 47403
www.authorhouse.com
Phone: 1-800-839-8640

Published by AuthorHouse   03/09/2012

ISBN: 978-1-4685-6050-3 (sc)
ISBN: 978-1-4685-6049-7 (hc)
ISBN: 978-1-4685-6048-0 (e)

Library of Congress Control Number: 2012904381

Follow my blog: http://shakin-not-stirred.blogspot.com
Follow me on twitter: @Alwaysshakin

To book David Chedester as a motivational speaker for any event, please contact: Summer Jo Brooks at summerjobrooks@gmail.com

This book was edited by Mark Damon Puckett—author of The Reclusives and YOU with The Ill-usives, available on amazon.com and bn.com

CONTENTS

To my family that helped me through everything in life,
and my new niece little Natalie

ACKNOWLEDGMENTS

I've got to say that writing this book has been one of the most important things I've ever done. Throughout writing this book, it has really served as a therapy for me. It's been a great way to relive all the things that I have gone through, and the impact they have had on my life. There are so many things still left that I want to accomplish, but getting this book published to raise money for Parkinson's Disease research is the most important. I think going through all of those bad times, and learning so much from them has taught me to look at the world in a different way. Now it's time to help encourage others to help me do that as well. Just like so many others that helped me along the way with this book.

I have to thank my parents first and foremost for bringing me into this world. Mom, you have always been there for me no matter what it was that I went through and I love you so much. Dad, you have been an unbelievable parent, role model, and friend. You've helped me so much on how to deal with having Parkinson's and I really hope that I can help with finding a cure for you and me. My older brother Clint and my older sister Lindsey—I love you both so much and am so glad that we had such an awesome time growing up together. All 5 of us have gone through so many difficult times, especially recently, but we've stuck together as a family through it all. I couldn't have asked for a better family in the whole world.

A special thanks goes out to the following people that really helped me along the way with this book and in my life: Mamaw, Aunt Lynnette, Uncle Mark, Brian Powell, Dr. Kinsey, Dr. Birch, Dr. Fame and your staff, Lisa Humble, Nicole and Natalie Bullano, Stu and Jade Spencer, Tom Lunsamnn, Thomas and Crystal Tacogna, Heather Wilson, Elizabeth Morgan, Diana Yu, Shante Ruffins, Dr. John Selman and his office staff, and my new baby niece Natalie Morgan Belcher. There are so many others that have helped me through this whole process, and just because I didn't name you in this book doesn't mean you weren't important to me. I wish my Granny and Papap would've been alive to help me go through this but I know they are always watching down on me.

PROLOGUE

My eyes slowly open after a long night of tossing and turning in my bed, as I go through another night of no sleep. I'm still very tired and could easily choose to lie in bed for a few more hours, but I have a big appointment at 7:45 a.m. that I can't miss. I've been anticipating this day for nearly 6 months. Most people would completely dread this day if they were in my shoes, yet I feel this is in a way going to be some closure for me. I'm up a little before 6:00, not because I want to be, but because my body gave me signs to wake up. I can feel my right hand, all the way up to my elbow, start to tremble a bit. This has been going on for almost a year now; however, it never used to shake all the way up to my shoulder. It usually was just a twitching sensation in my fingers that has progressed very quickly. I know at this point that if I want to be able to drink coffee comfortably, or even shave, that I've got to get up now and take some medicine.

I try to quickly get out of bed, which used to be a simple task has now become a struggle, especially since my balance is not what it used to be. So I managed to stumble onto the floor and march down the hallway, passing up the bathroom and ignoring the notion that I really need to piss. Now that my body knows that I'm awake, time is essential. In order for my hands and mouth to stop shaking, I am relying on a small yellow pill in my kitchen cupboard to relieve me. I know it will take at least 20 minutes for the pill to kick in; just the perfect amount of time for me to shower, shave, and get dressed with full cooperation from my hands and body. I know that once it starts working, I can live through a pretty normal start of the day. For the next 4 hours.

Once I get to the kitchen, I quickly fling open the refrigerator door and grab the first bottle of water that I see (knocking over a few bottles in the process). I stumble over to the kitchen cabinet that's just above the sink and pry open the door, accidentally banging it against the wall. Recently, my balance and coordination have really regressed because of my health situation; this will soon be much better once my little yellow miracle pill works its way through my system. I stare at the medicine bottle for a few seconds, knowing that it will take me a few tries before I can get the top open. I've tried to master this process for several months now, yet I still seem to have trouble. It sounds very simple to just pop the top off a medicine bottle, which for anyone else would be extremely simple.

Not for me.

After hundreds of different attempts at maneuvering my hands, altering my body, applying pressure with my legs, or whatever other style I've tried, I have finally found the right trick. My routine involves clinching the bottle tightly with my right hand (which makes my hand tremor even worse), then I place my left hand flatly on top of the bottle. At this point, it looks like I am trying to strangle the bottle to death; however, it's the only way I can ever get it to open. I end the battle by twisting as hard as I can until the bottle finally agrees to open up. It appears that this is a simple thing to do, although my hands aren't really cooperating with me this morning, and they usually don't any other morning. Lucky for me I get the bottle open on the first try, and as I always do, spill several pills on the counter and floor as I hurriedly throw one down my throat, chasing it down with water. I manage not to spill any water on me or the floor this time since I just took one big swig, not allowing the water bottle time to flip and fling around in my hand.

I take a deep breath, one of relaxation knowing that soon my body, my mouth, my balance, and my hands will be under control temporarily. I scoop up the pills that fell on the floor and one by one drop them back into the medicine bottle, clasp the top back and place it in the cabinet. I leave one pill out so that I can take it with me to work since I will have to take it again before lunch. This is a strategy I developed to not relive that morning session battle all over again before lunch. My first battle of the morning has been a huge success.

My next battle happens quickly right after: making coffee.

I love drinking coffee. I could drink it all day if it was at all healthy for me to do. Fresh ground coffee beans brewed in the morning combined with some hazelnut creamer, and I'm good to go. Just recently I had to cut out sugar from my coffee because it almost stops my medicine from working. Ever since I got turned on to grinding the beans myself, I've never gone back to instant coffee. This however does create a process that at times is a bit too much for me early in the morning. Too much coffee and caffeine for anyone typically gives them the shakes. For me, it only multiplies my problem by a factor of ten.

Pouring the beans into my grinder always results in a few beans ending up on the ground, and pouring the newly crushed coffee grounds into the coffee maker usually has the same spilling results. It hasn't always been like this for me, but within the past year, the simplest things have now become a challenge for me to do. I open up the coffee cabinet where all my necessities are stored, and I hope that one of the coffee filters is already separated so that I won't have the challenge of peeling one away from the stack of 200. To my dissatisfaction, there isn't one that's already loose. So, call it a challenge or battle, but the second battle is about to begin: separate 1 coffee filter and peel it away from the stack.

I grab a stack of 50 or so and throw it down on the counter hoping that a few will juggle loose from the stack. No luck. I hold the stack with my right hand tightly against my body and use my left index finger to try and pry one away. Attempt after attempt continues to fail, and I can't manage to get these filters seemingly unglued from each other. I don't know how they go about packaging those filters, because getting just 1 peeled away is not a fun part of my day. Finally after about 20 seconds, I manage to get 2 that are completely attached to each other peeled away from the stack. I'm not up to trying to separate the 2, so looks like I'm going to waste a filter today, which usually ends up happening every morning anyway.

Nevertheless, I win the battle against the coffee filters; finish getting the coffee ready; and flip the on switch so that it can brew while I take a shower. I have this routine perfected by now, knowing that once I am done showering and shaving, the coffee will be ready and my hands will be much more stable.

My morning at this point only gets better, with only one last challenge before my day gets started: locking my apartment door. This challenge weighs heavily on my head all morning as I get ready. My only hope is that none of my neighbors will be in the hallway to watch me try and fit the key perfectly into the key hole to lock the door. Try as I may to not think about the inevitable, I manage to go on about my morning.

Showering and shaving are easy for me now that my medicine has begun to kick in. Getting dressed in a suit and tie, which I wear every day, is easy for me right now as well, and this process goes unscathed without any struggles. I wonder for a split second at what point in my life that shaving, or even getting dressed, will be very hard for me to do on my own. These thoughts come and go. I never dwell on them or let them get me down. I'm living in the moment, every single moment, just enjoying where I am at.

I finish getting ready, take my dogs out for their morning business, and head back inside to the kitchen for my much deserved and much needed cup of joe. Because of the pill I took this morning, I know I can't eat for an hour; otherwise the medicine won't work. Instead, I have a cup of coffee at home to waste time before my bowl of oatmeal or cereal. Every time I pour my cup, I make sure to only fill it about 2/3 of the way, in order to drink what's in the cup and not spill it. Since I'm a bit nervous for my appointment, my hands are still a bit shaky even though the medicine is now working. Just taking a few deep breaths, letting the anxiety go away, I feel my nervousness disappearing. I finally start to feel at ease, and so does my body. My miracle pill has moved into full gear. I know the medicine is working because I place both hands up in the air, as if giving myself up to the police.

I just stare at them.

I'm amazed at how (almost) still they are.

It puts a huge smile on my face to know that for just a short while, my body appears to be normal. This doesn't mean that I can drink from a normal mug today. Since I know I'm about to leave, I already know I have to drink it with a lid on top, or my hands will be scorched with blazing hot coffee. I've learned to do this after numerous times of spilling hot coffee all over my hands and burning the hell out of them. In goes the coffee, along with a few heaping tablespoons of hazelnut creamer.

And my day is ready to get started.

YES! I managed to get my coffee put together without spilling much at all. Before I was on medicine, my counter would look like a construction zone of complete coffee destruction. Not anymore. A few drops of black coffee, a few coffee beans, and a splash of hazelnut lay on the counter from my small battles this morning. This is nothing that a paper towel can't clean up in one big swipe across the counter. Cleaning this doesn't take much concentration for my hands, so I shovel all the spilled mess into the garbage, throw away the paper towel, and pet my dogs for a few seconds before I walk out my front door.

I slowly crack the door open and peek out into the main hallway to make sure none of my neighbors is out. My appointment is only 4 miles away, and I still have about 10 minutes to burn before I have to be there. As I mentioned before, the pressure of having someone watch me lock my door is too much for me to handle. I have to make sure the hallway is empty before leaving. This way, if anyone is outside, I can act like I'm going to check my mail and not have strange eyes peering at me from a distance as I embarrassingly try to lock my door. I look both ways and my eyes light up because it's just me and no one else in the hallway. Today's a success because everyone must still be asleep, so I shut my front door and try quickly to lock it.

Failure already starts as it is taking me way too long to get the key in my hand, which leads to me dropping the keys on the floor. Now I can feel my hands really not wanting to cooperate with me. Maybe it's nerves or feeling pressure to hurry up and get the door locked; either way this is going to be tough. Even though I know I am all alone in the hallway, just the thought of someone walking out their door is crammed into my brain. This third battle of the morning is really starting to frustrate me because this simple task of locking my front door has now become a race against time. I'm just hoping that I can keep it together for 2 seconds and fit the key into the lock. I've learned to accept the fact that this will always take me 5 or 6 tries before I can finally get the door locked. But I've managed to have a little fun with it too. Sometimes if I get the key in within a few tries and lock the door, I will turn around and give a high five to the stairwell in front of me, mocking a bit of celebration, like I just hit a homerun in a baseball game.

I haven't let dropping the keys get my confidence down too much, and with a little luck, I manage to get the key into the lock on just my third attempt. While this would sound ridiculous for most people to take that many tries just to lock their front door, it happens to be a victory for me and my hands. This puts a huge smile on my face, and

I follow that up by giving my celebratory high five to the stairwell and mumble to myself, "It's gonna be a good day."

Today is my first day as a diagnosed patient diagnosed with Parkinson's Disease.

FLASHBACKS THAT I WILL NEVER FORGET

As I got into my car to drive off to my neurology appointment, I had a painful flashback that popped into my mind before my legs would even allow me to press on the gas pedal of my car. It was a clear picture in my mind that I will never forget, and I'm sure my father felt the exact same way. This was going to be a complete life-changing appointment for me, and all I could think about was a phone call I received my junior year of college, back in 2004 where I played baseball at Greenville College in Illinois. I had gotten a call from my mother telling me that Dad was at work and had back-to-back grand mal seizures on top of the mountains where he worked. My father was a Civil Engineer who worked all his life in the coal mines, as well as surveying land up in the mountains of Eastern Kentucky.

He worked extremely hard to provide for our family, but had an alcohol and drug addiction that he battled for nearly 30 years. Mom wasn't sure if he was going to be okay, but she did her best at assuring me that he would be fine. I took the news extremely hard because for the past few years leading up to his seizures, I hadn't had much of a relationship with him. Looking back on that period of time, I wish we would've been closer. Our family had fallen apart during my final 2years of high school, and I always held a grudge against him and my mother. While there is nothing more in the world I would do to take that time back to have a relationship with him; I can't. I was young and dumb. After talking with mom for a while, I made my way from

1

my dorm towards our indoor baseball practice facility. I met with our hitting coach, Brock Friese, later that day before practice to tell him the news, and that I had made the decision to walk away from baseball and school for a week to isolate myself from everyone. Coach Friese tried his best to talk me out of my decision, telling me that this was the time I needed my friends and teammates the most. However, I didn't take his advice, nor did I feel like having a lecture on how I should be acting responsibly. Coach also knew that I wasn't a religious person, but he did politely ask if he could pray for Dad and my family. I looked at him right in the face and wanted to strangle him.

"Coach, God doesn't exist. All these times we pray before and after practice and games, it means nothing. It never helps. If God was such this great person that you talk about, then why has he let this happen to my Dad? Why's he let this happen to me and my family? Oh yeah, some God he is."

Coach Friese sat and watched me go on this tirade for about a minute, until I finally finished acting like an idiot. He looked up at me and apologized for me feeling that way.

"David, I understand you're upset, and you can choose to stay in this room and listen to my pray or you can leave. Either way, I'm going to pray, and trust me,

God will listen."

This was the other thing that killed me. Here I was acting like a complete idiot, discriminating the MAN that all Christians believe in, and it had no effect on Coach at all. After listening to me say all that, he still wanted to pray. How could I walk out at that point?

So I sat across from Coach Friese with my head down, listening to him as he prayed for my dad and my family.

The room that we were in was Coach Carlson's office—Carlson was our head baseball coach. His office had a huge window on the left wall that overlooked our recreation center where we practiced during the winter months, or whenever it was raining outside. I just happened to peek out the window while Coach Friese was praying, and I saw the entire team kneeling down, hats off, as Coach Carlson lead a team prayer as well. This really moved me to see how quickly the team and coaches had gathered around to help me during this tragic time. I knew that Dad was a strong man but wasn't sure how he would respond to this tragic event. I knew Dad had been messed up on drugs and alcohol for a long time, and actually thought that his body just had enough. In the back of my mind, I wasn't sure I'd ever see my father again.

I spent nearly a week isolating myself from all my friends and teammates, only allowing my girlfriend at the time to see me. I drank heavily during that week, hoping to use the alcohol to help me escape from the problems that were going on. I was smarter than that to act in such a way, but I just wasn't mature or strong enough. I knew the alcohol would only be a temporary scapegoat at night, and the same problems would be awaiting me in the morning, along with a pounding headache.

I worried a lot about Mom and Dad during that week. They had split up during my senior year of high school and hadn't really spoken to each other much. In fact, I hadn't spoken to my Dad for a long time because of the anger I still had about them splitting up. I wondered if this situation, this emotional point of family tragedy would bring us together again, or push us farther apart. While it took many months for us to get closer and rally around Dad again as he slowly recovered, years later our family would again be decimated. After weeks of rest, he ended up being okay, but life for him and our family would be very rocky for the next year.

It was a true test for us, and yet we came together as a family, which should be what most families do. A little more than 16 months after Dad's seizure attack, he once again would go through another traumatic event in his life. He would receive news from a neurologist in Knoxville, Tennessee, that he never would have imagined hearing. He had developed Parkinson's Disease. Dad had been suffering from chronic fatigue for a few years, and he slowly developed a tremor in his right hand. That's what led to him seeking the advice of a neurologist. Parkinson's wasn't very familiar at all to me, nor anyone in our family. I had no clue what signs or symptoms came along with this disease, or if it was even life threatening. I just knew that when Mom called to tell me about it, I was very upset. I mean, who wouldn't be, right? Anytime you hear of someone being diagnosed with any illness, you always assume that it's something terrible or life-threatening. When Dad had the seizures, I was away at college, 10 hours from home, but I at least had my friends and baseball teammates/coaches to turn to for help. However, when Dad was diagnosed with Parkinson's, I was living in North Carolina, all alone, and had a tough time dealing with the news. It was almost as if God wouldn't leave our family alone.

Or at least that's how I felt at the time.

For all my life it just seemed as if the world was always shitting on me, and our family. With Dad having PD, this was just something else to add to a long list of misery that followed my life. I spent a few hours reading about the disease and educating myself about what it does to the body. Little did I know that not only did this effect the physical appearance of the body (constant tremors, mask face, difficulty walking), but it also led to clinical depression and anxiety. My father had lived such a tough life that I couldn't help but feel sorry for him after reading about Parkinson's.

But it was during Dad's early battle with Parkinson's that I recalled a few sentences from one of my college Anatomy & Physiology textbooks that made me fear that I was starting to develop the same illness that Dad had been diagnosed with. My appointment with a neurologist was because of the same symptoms Dad had developed when he was 50; chronic fatigue and a tremor in my right hand. These were 2 major symptoms that I read about in that book, along with another paragraph that shocked me. While I can't remember exactly how it was worded, I will just give you a paraphrase:

> *Scientists believe that while genes do play a part in developing Parkinson's Disease, they still aren't sure whether it's a major or minor role. If someone in the immediate family has developed Parkinson's Disease, than they have a significant increase in chance to pass the disease to their children. However, the Disease very rarely shows up before the age of 50. There are cases where the disease can show up at early ages, but it is extremely rare. It is also possible that a blow to the head causing any type of damage or trauma to the brain could trigger the symptoms of Parkinson's Disease. Person(s) can be born with pre-genetic disposition of having Parkinson's Disease, but an environmental factor or trauma to the brain must cause the disease to show up.*

My mouth stayed wide open as I continued reading on about the symptoms and what the chances were of my brother, sister, or I developing this disease. How old is the average person before they start to see signs of the disease? Will Parkinson's Disease cause death? Are there medications out there to prevent the disease from occurring? Is there even good medication to treat the symptoms? The questions kept popping up in my brain one after another so quickly that I could feel my heart racing, close to bursting out of my chest. I knew that Muhammad Ali had the disease, and that Michael J. Fox had recently come out saying he had the disease as well. Were Dad's symptoms going to get as bad as Ali's? If I had Parkinson's, is that what I would be like as I got older? What if I ever decided to have kids, or my brother or sister wanted them? What were the chances of them passing on the disease?

I couldn't stop the questions from piling up in my head. While I was extremely concerned about my father, I couldn't help but be scared for myself at the same time. My right hand had been slightly shaking for over 5 years, but I never went to see a doctor about it. Now that I had learned about Dad having the disease, the thought immediately popped into my head that I could have it as well. Dad was just over 50 years old when he started showing signs of Parkinson's.

I was only 18.

THE DOCTOR WILL SEE YOU NOW....

That day I was referring to in the prologue was a day that my life completely changed forever. It was a follow-up appointment with my doctor, but not just any doctor: my neurologist, Dr. J. Gordon Burch. He was a neurologist in Roanoke, Virginia, who came highly recommended by several doctors from around the area. I was seeing Dr. Burch because for the past 9 years of my life, I wasn't able to keep my hands from shaking. What had started out as a twitch in my right pinky slowly had progressed to my entire hand. Also, the tremors had progressed from my hand all the way up to my elbow. What worried me even more was that the tremors weren't just on my right side of the body, but both sides. Not only was I having hand tremors, my speech wasn't as clear as it always had been. Mom and Dad always bragged about me having the "gift of gab", but lately I wasn't able to respond to someone as quickly as I once did. I'd have what I wanted to say in my mind, then my lips and mouth wouldn't always cooperate with me to say anything. My balance wasn't what it used to be, and my photographic memory that professors at my college used to brag about to me had dwindled all the way to nothing. Recently there were even times where I couldn't remember what I had eaten for breakfast.

I recall a few times where I would be sitting in my recliner at my apartment, get up, walk into the kitchen and just stare with extreme confusion. I didn't even know why I had walked in there. During my college years I could've recited without a pause every muscle and bone in the human body without looking at a textbook or skeleton. Now I couldn't even read two sentences out loud without pausing or becoming confused.

I was really nervous about seeing Dr. Burch, so I spent the night before that appointment by myself at my apartment. I sat alone with computer in my lap, watching YouTube videos of inspirational speeches, trying to stay positive and build up some pride. For the past 5 months of trying several different medicines, eliminating the possibility of my condition being any number of diseases, Dr. Burch had finally nailed it with my first prescription of Sinemet (a combination of Carbidopa and Levodopa). This is without a doubt a drug that no one near my age should be on, but I had been taking it for 2 months and it really had made a huge impact on treating the symptoms I had been struggling with. Since I had called in for several refills on the medication, Dr. Burch moved up my next appointment to see him. This was because he knew the inevitable outcome and diagnosis due to the response my body was having with Sinemet. I had learned to accept what was going to come from that appointment though still had times when I struggled with the realization of what my life would now be like. I was extremely depressed that night, and had been battling depression for the last 7 months or so.

Any number of my friends or family seeing me over that time frame could probably tell you how clear it was that my life was in shambles.

I recall a conversation I had with my long time best friend from high school, Brian Powell, back in July of 2011. He knew that I had been seeing a neurologist for several months and was also aware of the disease I had been possibly battling. Brian has always been someone that I've respected. I spent a weekend with him up in Harrisonburg, Virginia, to relax and just enjoy the fun we always had. We've never failed to laugh our asses off when we were hanging out. Whether it was quoting funny movies, hiking, or going bowling, we never had a dull moment, except when we lost in the Regional Semifinals in high school baseball to our biggest rival. Nevertheless, while he and I were sitting around watching a movie, we started talking about our past. Most of the conversation consisted of talking about great moments that had happened in our lives, many of which were hilariously funny, and all of which involved alcohol. However, Brian wasn't near the drinker that I had been, or had recently become for that matter. Yeah, we both were known to throw back some beer and have fun, but he never went overboard to the extent of how bad I drank. Brian and I had become much closer friends over the past year (2010) and he was one of my true friends witnessing me drink myself into oblivion.

He ended up asking me a question that weekend that I never wanted to hear.

Brian and I were talking about our careers, things we wanted to accomplish in life, and somehow got on the topic of drinking. All throughout college I drank, and even up to that weekend I had drunk all my life since I graduated from college in 2005. I wasn't a binge drinker, so I thought, but on the weekends I definitely drank a lot. Now that I had fallen into a bit of depression (staring a rare disease in the face at 27), I had been drinking every day. I tried to always be positive about my situation, but spending countless nights alone usually resulted in my positive attitude being drowned in a bottle of vodka, only to leave me feeling a lot of sorrow and resentment for my situation. In fact, from January of 2010 until late September of 2011, I drank every day. I was downing a liter of vodka every 2 days. There were numerous mornings where I'd wake up on my couch and not realize where I was or what had happened the night before. I was so scared of having Parkinson's and so pissed that I couldn't get my hands to stop shaking, that I again was using alcohol to run from my problems. Besides, when I was drunk, it was the only time my hands stopped shaking, and I got some kind of strange joy out of that. Here I was, hanging out with Brian, trying to tell him that I had accepted my (possible) disease and was fine with it, but deep down inside I really wasn't. I knew it, and to an extent, so did Brian. After he watched me throw back a 6 pack of beer and several shots of vodka, without hesitation, he asked me, "You don't think you have a drinking problem, do you?"

For God's sake I had been drinking since I was 12 years old, which meant that for over 15 years I had spent relying on alcohol for any number of reasons. Never once in my mind had I ever thought I had a problem. I laughed off his question and quickly spouted out a "No." I didn't want to admit it to anybody, but deep down inside I knew I was lying. During those 5 months of trial and error with trying different medications to narrow down the long list of diseases that I might have, I drank heavily every night. Even the night before one of the most important, life-defying appointments of my existence, I drank. I never really had the thoughts of "why me" when it came to seeing Dr. Burch time after time. I just never thought that at the age of 27 I would need to see a neurologist on a regular basis.

I drank heavily that night before Dr. Burch diagnosed me—to try and calm my nerves. It didn't work. I distinctively remember at one point to pour a glass of vodka and diet ginger ale. My hands wouldn't let me. I tried just using my right hand to pour the ginger ale in my glass. It shook and spilt all over the counter. Even when trying to control the 2-liter bottle with both hands, it shook and spilled even more. My shaking had never truly been this bad, but whenever I got nervous, the symptoms worsened. I spent more time that night cleaning up spilt vodka and ginger ale then I actually did drinking it. I knew this was stupid of me to drink THE NIGHT BEFORE GOING TO SEE A NEUROLOGIST, but I was in such a state of intense depression and denial that I knew the alcohol would eventually help put my mind and nerves to rest, and help me eventually pass out.

Sadly, not even the alcohol helped me sleep that night, as I tossed and turned and listened to my dogs Saytii and Maddie snore lying next to me. I might have gotten 30 minutes of sleep that night but that's probably even a bit of a stretch. It seemed like I just lay there and stared at the ceiling just waiting for the sun to come up because I was so worried about what Dr. Burch was going to say to me.

The morning going to see Dr. Burch had definitely started out in a positive note since I succeeded in locking my front door on just a few attempts. Semi-triumphantly, I gave my routine high five to the stairwell. As anxious as I was to talk with Dr. Burch, I was also a bit scared because this was my fourth appointment with him, and I always went by myself. I knew this would be the hardest one to go to alone. I had wanted to go alone yet also hated the fact that I was going through this at such a young age, without a family or even a girlfriend to help support me.

I remember reading both of Michael J. Fox's books where he talked about his experience of going through this same process, and I admired the fact that he had such a great wife and family to help him through his diagnosis of Parkinson's Disease. There were so many times where it made me think of previous relationships I'd had, that only if they had worked out, then maybe I would have a supportive wife to help me go through this. But I didn't, and I knew that it was going to be the toughest pill for me to swallow. I mean, I am sure there are lots of people my age, and even younger that have to see neurologists on a regular basis, and most of them have to be seen for far worse reasons than me. But then again, everyone always thinks that whatever illness they have is the worst possible thing that anyone could have. I was never one to think like that. I always had the feeling of, ok, whatever I have, I can't take it back. I am just going to have to live with it the best I can.

I had been through so many horrible things throughout my life that I wouldn't ever let some illness control my life or my attitude. But I have to admit, I was still very scared. I know at most doctors' offices you typically wait forever before you are called back, leaving you plenty of time to ponder and dwell upon all the horrible possibilities of news that's waiting on you. Not with Dr. Burch. As soon as I signed in that morning and paid my co-pay, I was prepared to at least sit down for a few minutes and calm myself down. But, I never got that chance. I took a half of a step away from the "sign-in" window only to hear: "David, Dr. Burch will see you now."

My heart immediately started racing.

This was it.

I had now been taking Sinemet for almost 2 months and it had really helped me start living as normal of a life as possible for someone in my situation. This is a drug that is designed to help with only 1 disease and, basically, if the drug is given enough time to stay in your system and helps with your symptoms, then it can only indicate the diagnosis of the disease it is used to treat: Parkinson's. At this point, I didn't even need Dr. Burch to tell me the diagnosis, because I already knew what the answer was.

Up to this very moment, I had done a pretty good job living a regular day-to-day life to keep my mind off of everything. I still continued working during the day and going to the gym at night. But once I was home alone, I popped open a bottle of vodka and wouldn't stop until I was blacked out. I did pretty much whatever I could to not worry about going to this appointment. As the nurse and I walked towards the patient room, my heart felt like it was going to jump out of my throat. I sat alone in the room for only a minute or two and, suddenly, I heard someone grab the chart that was sticking out of the little cubby attached to the outside of my room.

I knew it had to be Dr. Burch.

I started getting nervous as I knew he was reading all the notes from the previous times I had gone to see him. My heart continued pounding so hard against my chest that I held both hands against it, trying to keep it from busting through my skin. I sat there and wondered what was going through Dr. Burch's mind, especially since he had told me previously that he'd never had a patient at my age showing symptoms of Parkinson's Disease, and he had been a neurologist for over 30 years.

The door slowly opened up and in came one of the only people I was always very symptomatic around; mainly because I was nervous. Dr. Burch smiled at me and stuck out his hand for a good old-fashioned hand shake before we both sat down. I was scared to hold my hand out and wait for his to grab mine, only because leaving my hand out in the open like that for a few seconds displays my hand's inability to stop moving. I jerked my hand out of my pocket to give him a quick shake and shoved it right back into my pocket, almost like we had just exchanged a quick drug deal.

Now I have mentioned that the medicine works very well at keeping my tremors to a minimum, but when I am nervous or anxious, the medicine doesn't work as well. As I sat down, I kept both hands in my pocket just because I didn't want Dr. Burch to see me shaking nervously. While I can't speak for him, I knew that the next 10 or 15 minutes were going to be the most serious conversation of my life. I'm sure Dr. Burch had experienced many encounters just like we were about to have, but never with someone anywhere near as young as I was.

He started out by summarizing everything that we had talked about over the past 3 appointments, everything from what problems he thought I was experiencing, and the different medications we had experimented with. I shared my story about my family history of illnesses which included 2 relatives with Parkinson's, trauma to my brain from college baseball, and my inability to stop my hands from shaking, which were all things Dr. Burch and I had talked about before. Most experiences I had with doctors meant me doing a lot of talking while they sat and scribbled some notes on my chart, wrote me a prescription for medicine, and out the door they'd go. This wasn't the case at all with Dr. Burch. He was genuinely a great doctor, and even more so, actually cared about the situation I was currently facing. He had been a superlative doctor to me ever since I saw him for the first time back in early April of 2011. While I should've gone to see him in January of 2010 when the symptoms were progressing, I was just too scared to face the facts of what my body was going through. During previous visits, he talked to me at length about what he thought I could have, which was "essential tremors". An essential tremor merely means "that your hands start to tremor and never stop." They can be anything from just a twitching sensation in a few fingers to your hand or entire arm shaking, but no other symptoms. I knew this couldn't be the problem because of the other symptoms I was experiencing. Dr. Burch also talked about me having "Parkinsonian tremors" during another appointment, which just involve having the tremors, and another symptom or two, but not the actual disease state. He then went on to tell me about patients he had seen in the past experiencing similar symptoms that I had, and eventually became diagnosed with Parkinson's Disease, although never anyone my age. Even those patients he referred to had taken years of doctors' visits and evaluations before the actual diagnosis was given. Those had been previous conversations that we had over the past 5 months, but treatment for both essential and Parkinsonian tremors had failed. Ever since I had begun having success with Sinemet, the same medication that my father had been taking for almost 5 years, Dr. Burch and I were left with the only disease that I could possibly have: Parkinson's Disease.

For the past 9 years, I had been living with the thought that this day would eventually come, and I had run from this because I was so scared. I mean the possibility of someone my age being diagnosed with Parkinson's Disease was without a doubt one of the rarest conditions a person could have. I would dare to say that someone at the age of 27 would have a better chance of winning the lottery back-to-back days and being struck by lightning the next day, than to be diagnosed with Parkinson's. Just the very thought of my tremors beginning at the age of 18 could be enough cause to say my condition and disease began at that age. Unfortunately, Parkinson's is one of the most difficult diseases to diagnose because of the lack of knowledge and research that has been done with this illness. I've always applauded and admired Michael J. Fox and Muhammad Ali because of the amount of money they have both raised for Parkinson's research. While the money their foundations have raised is extremely significant, it's still managed to not be enough for researchers and scientist to discover a cure. The breakthroughs that have been made due to their contributions are mind-boggling and inspiring, but unless more money continues to come in for research, then this disease will continue to become more prevalent.

So, instead of seeing a doctor when my symptoms first started in 2002, I just went about life ignoring all the signs that something might be wrong with me.

Only I couldn't ignore it anymore.

Which is what led me to that day, August 22, 2011, with Dr. Burch when I was finally diagnosed with Parkinson's Disease.

After listening to Dr. Burch recap our last few visits and failed attempts with different medications, he immediately asked, "Now that you have been on Sinemet for several months now, how has it been working?"

I smiled for a few seconds before I answered, only because I had been very pleased with how my symptoms had been doing much better since I began taking the medication.

"I've been doing great. My tremors are far less obvious, almost to the point where my right arm and hand tremors have been minimized to just a twitching sensation in my fingers. My speech has gotten much better, so that the slurred and slowed speech that I had before is completely gone. And most of all, my handwriting has gotten a lot better."

"That's great David," Dr. Burch replied, "so what you're telling me is that the Sinemet is really working well for you?"

"I'm telling you Dr. Burch it's been a miracle drug for me. Some of the side effects early on weren't too pleasing, like the nausea, upset stomach, and sometimes I would get extremely drowsy right after I took it. But now that the artificial dopamine [the main chemical in Sinemet that helps treat symptoms associated with Parkinson's] has been in my system for a while, the side effects are nearly nonexistent lately."

"Ok, that's really great David that the side effects have gone away, which is a great sign. It shows your body is really starting to respond well to the Sinemet. I'm glad things are getting better for you, but now we've gotten to a point where I think you need to be evaluated more. Obviously I say this because of your age. It's such a rarity for anyone at your age to have Parkinson's Disease and we need to decide on what to do next."

After hearing Dr. Burch say this, I had a feeling of grief and shock because over the past year or so, I had convinced myself that I most likely had Parkinson's. Actually *hearing* those words from my neurologist, though, were a bit emotional. Even worse, the next two options that he offered to me were even more upsetting.

"David, at this point, I think we have 2 choices for you to decide on. The first option would be to go get evaluated at University of Virginia Medical Center by a movement disorder specialist, as well as a team of neurologists in order to get some final confirmation on what's going on with you. This is a great road to go down especially because it's one of the top medical centers in the U.S. and it's close to you geographically. The other option would be to go with my initial instinct that we have talked about before, and send you up to the best neurologist in America up in New York at Mount Sinai Hospital."

At this point, the easy decision would have been to go to UVA Hospital in Charlottesville, Virginia, merely because it was only 2 hours from Roanoke, where I was currently living. And they had one of the top medical facilities in the country, just as Dr. Burch had stated. However, I truly felt deep down inside that I needed the best of the best. I had talked at length with my father about what I should do, and he agreed with Dr. Burch's second suggestion, which was for me to go see the best neurologist in the United States. I had spent a lot of time thinking about what the right decision would be, and the choice ended up being a pretty easy one that morning.

"Well Dr. Burch, I've spoken with my father at length about this, and we both feel that going up to Mount Sinai Hospital is the best thing for me at this point in my life."

"I agree with you David. Your situation is very, very unusual—again, because of your age, and this is definitely a case where they are going to want to see you up there as soon as possible. I will make the phone call later this afternoon to get you set up and we will touch base in a week and go over everything . . . . does that sound good to you?"

"Sounds great, Dr. Burch, and thank you very much for doing this for me."

Luckily for me, Dr. Burch was not only a great neurologist, but one of his great friends just happened to be the #1 neurologist in the United States. Dr. Burch listed off a number of accolades that his friend had accomplished in the field of neurology, and that he had even served as head of the neurosurgery department at a top hospital in Italy. While I had some level of comfort knowing that I would be seeing the best doctor possible, I was also very scared at what else this neurologist would be evaluating me for, and if he might end up finding out that something else was wrong with me.

Over the past 5 months I had tried my best to stare the possibility of having Parkinson's in the face and convince myself that I was going to be ok. While I felt, up to this point, that I had done a good job of staying positive, I was actually hurting very deeply. Night after night ended up being the same for me, drinking a lot of beer and vodka, using it as a scapegoat from reality.

But reality had just come to the surface with no escape.

What had started out as dreading that I had the disease had now become truth, with no cure in sight. And on top of that, I now had to go see the most well known neurologist to see what *else* might be wrong.

I remember leaving Dr. Burch's office and driving home with just a complete blank stare on my face, not knowing what lay ahead for me in the next few weeks. I had accepted the fact that Parkinson's was going to be part of my life forever, and was fine with that. I always felt like it could've always been something worse, some other more dreaded disease that could be fatal, but Parkinson's isn't. I was always a tough and strong person, so I felt like Parkinson's was just another speed bump in my life. The only rough part was that I didn't have a companion to be there with me through the hard times.

I was very sad during the short drive home because I wasn't going to be greeted by anyone at the door to give me a big hug and tell me everything was going to be okay. There wasn't anyone there to sit down with me and share my emotions or tears and to tell me I was a strong person and was going to make it through this. That's what I really wanted, but I knew it wasn't going to happen. When I got home, I stared at my front door for several seconds before I eventually opened it up and slammed it shut, creating an extremely loud sound and echo throughout the hallway. At this point I wasn't sure if I was upset, or sad, or disappointed. I think I was just embarrassed with myself and the way I had reacted to everything that had been going on for the past 18 months. I knew I should've been smarter than to drink so heavily to avoid the very moment I was about to have. There wasn't a thing I could do at this point to stop what was happening to me, and until I TRULY learned that I was going to be okay with having Parkinson's, then my life would continue to be destroyed. My body felt at such a state of disarray and weakness that my keys fell out of my hand and made a loud clank as they hit the hardwood floor. I made it about 4 footsteps towards my bedroom before I completely collapsed to the floor, falling against the hallway wall and bowing my head between my legs. My excessively shaking hands tried to cover my face the best they could, but there wasn't a reason for them to do so because I was all alone. As hard as I tried to hold everything back, I had finally broken down. I completely lost it emotionally and was lying down without an ounce of energy in my body to get back up. That day I was diagnosed with a neurological disorder that would progressively continue to take control over my entire body, and I had no one to help me.

As I cried, all alone, I could only get out one sentence, and I just kept repeating it, "Who's gonna want me now?"

WAS THIS HOW IT HAPPENED?

I experienced many times in my life where I felt sorry for myself, just like I did when I wondered if anyone would want me since being diagnosed with Parkinson's Disease. One of the worst was when I went through a rough time in high school as I watched cancer take my Granny away from me. The following few years after Granny passed away, that downward spiral hit me. I started drinking for the first time, but not just having a few beers, drinking very heavily. I spent many nights passing out on the floor, be it in my bedroom or at one of my friends' houses. I had a hard time controlling myself because of how much pain and anguish I was feeling. My junior and senior years of high school are a total blur for me because my life was so out of control. I knew that if I wanted things to get better for me, I had to get away from my hometown and go to college far away from Eastern Kentucky. I needed a fresh start; a chance to turn my life around and become a better person. I knew if I didn't get away, my life would become ruined by alcohol. It's unfortunate that most people choose to never get away from the town that I grew up in and venture out somewhere else for college or to live. I had to get away, and that's exactly what I ended up doing. A few weeks before my 18th birthday, I packed up everything that I owned into my little '96 Nissan Sentra, and headed on a long 11-hour journey to my new hometown, Greenville, Illinois.

I was a freshman at Greenville College, a small Christian college about 45 miles east of St. Louis. I stupidly chose to go there because it was the only school that gave me enough money to cover the cost of all my expenses and play baseball. I say stupidly because it was a very religious school that based its education around faith and God, and I did not share nearly the same ideas. I just wanted to play baseball. I did get a few baseball scholarships from other small schools, but they were all very close to home and I knew that if I didn't get out of the small town in Kentucky where I went to school, then I'd never make it out of there. The only reason I even knew of Greenville College was because during the summer before my senior year of high school in 2000, I was at the University of Kentucky "Junior Day" baseball camp and Greenville's head baseball coach was there. This was a 3-day camp where some of the best high school baseball players around the state of Kentucky were invited to come practice, show off their talent and skills, and play in scrimmages in front of over a dozen college baseball coaches. While I wasn't nearly 1 of the top baseball players in the state, I was being softly recruited by Kentucky, which is why they extended the invitation to me. Or maybe because the top 200 players in the state turned down the choice, and they got around to player #245 and that happened to be me. Either way, I was grateful for the opportunity and that ended up being a pivotal choice that completely changed my life. Greenville's baseball coach, Lynn Carlson, was one of the coaches there to help out with the camp and teach different drills. He had earned his master's degree from the University of Kentucky and was looking for any type of talent that wasn't capable of playing at a top Division 1 school like Kentucky. That was me. I wasn't that great of a player. I was a decent pitcher, but just happened to be coached by one of the greatest high school baseball coaches of all time: Coach Billy Powell. He somehow had mastered the ability to take average baseball players and turn them into a great player. I wished I had gotten to play for him all through high school, but only got my senior year for him to coach me. On my best day, I could probably hit about 87 miles per hour, which for high school is pretty good, but when it comes to playing Division I baseball, unless I threw the ball underhand, side-armed, with movement, I'd just end up sitting the bench and keeping the score book for 4 years. But, Coach Madison, the head coach at Kentucky during that time, still invited me to the camp. Long story short, I strained my right ankle the first night I was there and my skills (what few I had) were completely limited. This meant pitching was completely thrown out the window, and I'd have to rely on my "average at best" hitting skills.

Even with being injured, I ended up having a decent camp, and started getting recruited by Greenville College and a few junior colleges from Indiana and Ohio. I actually met Coach Carlson inside the dorm room all the players were staying during the camp. I was in one of the recreation rooms watching WWF wrestling and in walks this 6'6", 250—pound giant and says hi to me, then tells me to turn it to ESPN because wrestling is fake and boring. My first thought was, "Who is this idiot!"

In 2000, the WWF was the biggest thing since sliced bread! Are you serious, Stone Cold Steve Austin, The Rock, Triple HHH . . . need I say more! Since I knew he was one of the recruiters there, I turned it to ESPN and we sat back and watched baseball highlights for about 30 minutes. All during this time he was telling me about Greenville College, their baseball team, the campus, and also mentioned the idea that it was a Christian-affiliated college, and that I would live a Christ-like life. As soon as those words came out of his mouth, the next thing I thought was, "I'd rather be dead than go there."

I was never a very religious person at all; in fact, I had been listening to Marilyn Manson a lot at that time, since this happened to be in the beginning of my rebellion time. I tried the whole religion and prayer thing during my sophomore year of high school when Granny got sick, and that didn't help. So, since I was young, I blamed God and Christ for the death of Granny and turned into a rebel. All my life I was told you have to do this, you have to do that, you have to live this kind of life, you're not allowed to do this, pretty much what a lot of us are told.

Don't drink. Don't do drugs. Don't cuss. Don't stay out past curfew or you're grounded. Basically, you're told to do all the things that equate to being a "good person" and not to do anything that was against the "norm". I mean my parents never were really like that, but other people involved around my life were. Listening to Manson was my way of escaping. And, to this day, I follow his music, his art, read his books, buy his CD's, and I have gone to his concerts. When Coach Carlson said "Christ-like life", I thought of Manson and the fact that there was no way I would ever go there. However, I researched their college, and the baseball team was actually pretty good. After fielding many phone calls from him and other players on the team during my senior year of high school, I signed a letter of intent to play baseball at Greenville College in the fall of 2001.

I figured that since baseball took up so much time, and most baseball players are pretty cool and laid back, that there would be some guys there I could relate to. However, with college baseball, I was shocked at how much more time you had to devote to the sport than what I ever did in high school. Hours and hours every day were dedicated to either practice, working out, or extra hitting drills. Since I was there to be a pitcher and play first base, I had double duties of working out with the pitchers and hitters, on top of going to school to get an education. Although I was a much better pitcher than I was a hitter, I still loved just playing the game. During fall baseball season, most of the practices during the week ran about 3 hours, then on Saturday, we typically held intersquad scrimmages. It was during one of these scrimmages in September, our annual Black vs. Orange World Series Games, that my life would be changed forever.

I was one of 12 freshmen on that incoming class and we were usually the guys having to carry around the equipment, clean up after practice, pretty much all the stuff that none of the upperclassman had to do because they'd already paid their dues. I always acted so cocky during practice because I thought I was hot stuff when it came to pitching. Now looking back on it, I was a pretty good player, but nowhere good enough to be as cocky as I was. As a pitcher, I had finished with 9 wins and 2 losses my senior year at Middlesboro High School, on a team that went 28-11. I had a fastball that had a lot of movement, a decent curveball, but my best pitch was my circle change-up. Coach Powell, my baseball coach at Middlesboro, whom I still love chatting with to this day, taught me how to throw it. When I perfected it, man, that pitch was my go-to pitch.

I still remember a game against Louisville Male High School, which had about 2,300 students, compared to the mere 400 at Middlesboro, where I threw 73 of 85 pitches that were circle change-ups. To this day, Brian Powell, who has been one of my best friends for over a decade, argues that there's no way this was true, but I still believe it to be. What's funnier is that his younger brother Vince was the catcher that game. And I swear if I had a dollar for every time Vince signaled the number 3 with his fingers (which meant to throw the circle change-up) I'd have 73 dollars, and would gladly throw them in Brian's face to prove him wrong. Well, the best thing about that pitch is that I could make it drop anywhere from 6 to 8 inches. The other great part is that a good change-up makes your fastball seem even faster than what it truly is, which I needed since I didn't really throw very hard. But, for Division III baseball, which was what Greenville was, 87 miles per hour was very good. So I thought I was a big shot. So, on an extremely hot Saturday early afternoon, we were in the middle of another Black vs. Orange scrimmage, which tended to get pretty heated between both teams. It was called the Black vs. Orange World Series because our team colors were Black and Orange. Young, cocky, a little overweight and 17 years old, I was told by Coach Carlson to warm up because I was going to pitch the next inning.

I went into the bullpen with Kris Zalman, another freshman who ended up being one of my best friends in college and one of the funniest guys I'd ever met. I warmed up. Several minutes later, our team made its third out hitting, and it was my time to go in. I didn't know a whole lot about the team at the time because we had only been practicing for a few weeks. I *did* know that our shortstop, Kyle Schultz, was a stud. He had been an All-Conference player twice, was captain of the team, and just an unbelievable athlete. What was even more admirable about him was that he was twice as good of a person than he was a baseball player. Kyle was the ideal son that all parents would want to call their own. At this time though, I didn't know how great of a hitter he REALLY was. During these scrimmages, hitters were videotaped so that we could watch ourselves and our hitting approach. As baseball players, we are usually obsessed at watching videotape of our swing in slow motion, and the same goes for pitchers, because this is the only way to see what we do well, and where we need to tweak what we are doing wrong.

During this scrimmage, I was on the mound, my friend Darius Jackson was catching, and the first hitter that I would be facing was Kyle Shultz, or, as we all called him, Shultzy. The videotape was set up in our home dugout in a position that it would get the best view of every hitter, starting from their stance, and all the way through his swing. It was aimed in close enough that you almost could see me from the pitcher's mound, but I was just out of the camera view. Darius and Shultzy had been teammates for 4 years now, which meant Darius knew how good a hitter he was. This was about to be my first pitch during an intersquad scrimmage, and boy was I nervous but extremely excited at the same time. I wanted to show off my 2-seam fastball that had tailing movement. Since I didn't throw extremely hard, having movement on my fastball was very important. This was another thing Coach Powell had taught me. If my arm motion was at a certain angle, and I put a certain amount of pressure with the tip of my index and middle finger on the seams of the ball, it would move inward toward the hitter, making the ball very difficult to hit squarely. However, Darius knew that Shultzy could hit any fastball, which led to him calling for a first pitch change-up, which I've already said was my best pitch. I am not sure Darius knew this at the time, but he probably called it to save me the embarrassment of Shultzy lining a double into the outfield gap. Stupidly, and cocky, I shrugged off the change-up. Through years and years of being a pitcher, I had never once in my life shrugged off throwing my change-up. Darius paused for a moment, looked down, and then flashed the sign for a fastball, the old number 1. I nodded my head letting Darius know that the fastball was coming. I moved the ball around in my glove a few times and got my two seam grip with my fingers, stared down at Darius's glove and took a deep breath.

Here came my very first pitch during a scrimmage as an official college baseball player.

I started my motion, kicked my left leg up and threw my fastball as hard as I could. Less than about 1 second later, I lay unconscious on the pitcher's mound. Shultzy had hit the ball as squarely on the fat part of the bat as possible, and it connected with the right temple of my head, barely missing the orbital bones around my right eye. I was actually lucky because if I hadn't moved my head to the right by a few centimeters, the ball could have hit me in my right eye destroying my eye socket, breaking bones, and possibly leaving me blind. Remember me saying earlier that there was a videotape rolling, taping every hitter's at-bat?

That entire 1 pitch at-bat that I just described happened in less than 4 seconds. I have seen the video played several times and the sound that is made when the ball connected with my temple sounded even louder than the sound of the crack of the ball as it connected with Shultzys' EASTON Red Zone bat. Before the video shuts off, all that you can hear was the ball hit my head, and Coach Carlson scream out "OH GOD!" After probably 30 seconds or so, I came to, and everything around me was spinning, like I was stuck inside a tornado.

The first person I saw was Coach Carlson staring at me with the look of disbelief that I was even alive. The entire team was also surrounding me as well. I don't remember a whole lot about that moment, but I do remember hearing some of the seniors laughing in the background. Mike, our athletic trainer, was there next to me looking around my temple and eye to see what type of damage had been done. He held his finger up and made me follow it to test me for a concussion, but the more he had me hold my head still and follow his finger with my eyes, the more it made me want to faint. I could feel my eyes cross every other second, almost as if I couldn't even control where they needed to go. After a few attempts at following his finger, I grabbed his hand and told him to stop. I just wanted off the field and to be somewhere safe; where no baseball could come close to hitting me. A few teammates helped pick me up and carried me to the dugout where I sat alone with a huge ice pack on my head. I had never experienced pain like this before in my life. It was soon afterwards that Morgan Spencer, a senior on the team, who later turned out to be another one of my best friends, drove me to the hospital for further tests to be done on my skull and brain.

The MRI and CAT scan thankfully showed no damage to my brain; I was diagnosed with a concussion and given a prescription for Vicodin. I still don't recall much of that day, or the days proceeding, but while sitting in the dugout about a week later, I noticed something wrong with my right hand.

My fingers wouldn't stop twitching.

No matter what I did, no matter how hard I concentrated on trying to keep them still, it just got worse. At the time I just thought it was just some nerve damage from the line drive I took off my head. I had shown our athletic trainer my fingers twitching and he just shrugged it off the same way I did. I just assumed after the concussion symptoms were gone away after a few weeks that the twitching would stop as well.

As the following days passed, my head started to feel better, and I went back to practice. However, my right hand still twitched. Another week passed, I was back to practice as usual, checking my right hand before every practice, only to continue to see my fingers twitch and soon watch it shake.

At this point, I started to worry why this wouldn't stop. After the concussion, I just wondered why my hand was shaking. Now, I wondered why my hand wouldn't stop shaking at all, and in fact got slightly worse. Was this typical after having such trauma to the head? Was this something that usually happened after suffering a concussion? So many questions were left unanswered in my head for many years as I continued to just shrug off the shaking. I never would've imagined it possible at the age of 18, but this was just an early sign that the shaking would never stop again, only to grow worse. I knew that I needed to see a doctor but was afraid of what I might find out. Instead of trying to get help, I did the one thing I always knew would put my mind at ease and help me relax.

I drank.

I didn't just drink though, I would binge drink until the point of blacking out most nights. I'd say for the final 3 years of college there might have been a total of 10 nights where I wasn't out partying until 3 or 4 in the morning. I was drinking heavily to not only have fun, but to run away from all the problems that were going on in my life. It was something that would continue to haunt me for the next 10 years of my life. My father was an alcoholic, along with almost all the other males in our family, which meant the chances of me becoming one were very high. I ignored the fact that it was happening to me because after all, doesn't everyone party in college? Well maybe not everyone, but I would venture to say that most people do. No one, however, was drinking as hard or as much as me. I was slowly killing my liver, brain, and more importantly: myself. But there was nothing I could do to stop it.

YOU CAN'T LEARN UNLESS YOU MAKE MISTAKES

I remember many times in my life where it seemed like things couldn't get any worse, especially during my college years and thereafter. I had many of those moments with my college sweetheart, Rachel, but had great times with her as well. If I wouldn't have been an immature/cocky/narcissistic/asshole, we would probably be married by now, with kids, a house, and a family pet or two. That seemed to be our plan all along. I mean we dated for over 3 years and told each other "I love you" after only dating for 4 months. She meant the world to me, and I to her, sadly we were just too young and stubborn to overcome many of our problems. I made so many mistakes throughout our time together, that I can't believe she put up with me in the first place.

She was far too pretty to date someone like me. I guess there was something about me that she just couldn't get enough of. I loved just lying in bed with her, cuddling. We spent so many nights like this. Truth be told, she was the first girl that I really enjoyed just lying with. That feeling of just holding each other, knowing that no matter what was going on outside of her bedroom, whatever horrible things were going on in the world, nothing else mattered. It was just us. She probably never knew that I never cared for someone as much as I did for her; somehow I had a horrible way of showing it. As bad as I made our relationship seem, and as many drunken fights as we had, we for the most part were always happy. We were the "main couple" of our small college I guess you could say. I don't say this meaning that we were the king and queen of dating; we were just always involved with drama and our college had less than 1200 students. Everyone knew us and everyone liked us. I was captain of the college baseball team and she was captain of the dance team. Parties were either at my house or her apartment, mostly. We were in college just living it up, having the time of our lives, without a care in the world.

The first time I knew she had strong feelings for me was when I left for the summer after my sophomore year of college. My brother was in the Navy, stationed down in Charleston, South Carolina, and he wanted me to spend the summer with him since we hadn't really seen each other in years. For most of my sophomore year, Rachel and I spent every waking moment together. Many times it was sneaking her into my dorm room, which always seemed to be an adventure in itself. When it came time for her to hug me goodbye for the summer, she completely broke down. I had never seen her like this. I mean, I had watched girls cry in front of me, which was just silly high school drama. The feeling I got from Rachel was that we had grown to be a great couple and she didn't want me to leave at all. I have to admit, that feeling was completely mutual. For the first time in my life, I was in love. I just wasn't smart enough to keep her. I graduated a year before her, and moved on to North Carolina to live with my sister and her future husband, Steve. And I guess that ended up being the demise for Rachel and me, because not too long after that, it was over between us. The way I ended it with her couldn't have been more horrible.

She came down to visit me for a week while I was helping out with this amateur baseball team, managing the beer deck at the stadium. She would come and drink for free while I would be at work, and I kept noticing that she looked to be gaining a little bit of weight. I always wanted a girl with a great body; that's how materialistic I was at the time. While I was working with the team, I had fallen for another girl: Megan. She, just like Rachel, was FAR too hot to be with someone like me. I mean this girl could've been in *Playboy*. She was galactically gorgeous. She ended up being the reason that I left Rachel. So, instead of being a man about it, and breaking up with her . . . . I simply changed my cell phone number and that was that. She tried and tried to get in touch with me. She called my parents, called my sister; she even called my Mamaw. I never did tell her that it was over.

What a sad excuse of a man I had become.

All those years that I invested into our relationship and staying committed to her, I couldn't even bring myself to end things with her. What kind of person does that? Who in their right mind just changes their phone number and immediately starts dating another girl? I was a disgrace. I couldn't even muster up enough happiness to put a smile on my face for months. Why should I? I wasn't a man. I wasn't anything. I was a lowdown piece of shit. Even after 4 years of college and a long term relationship, I had learned nothing about how to be a man, or how to be mature. Just looking back on how I was makes me want to go back in time and smack myself upside the head. But, I guess if we never make mistakes in life, we won't ever have a way of learning how to do things the right way, or how to become a better human being.

My time with Megan was short, which I figured would happen. We didn't even date for 2 months before we were broken up. She just wasn't right for me. We did have fun together at times, but our relationship was pretty much a joke. To no surprise, after Megan and I broke up, I tried running back to Rachel for months. Good thing for her, she never once took me back. Our phone conversations mainly consisted of her telling me how bad of a person I was and that she deserved far better than what I could give her. She kept reminding me how she wanted someone to treat her like a lady and make her smile again. Those were things that I just couldn't do for her anymore, and she wasn't ever going to take me back. I have to say I didn't blame her. She wanted to be happy and find someone that was better for her, and she later did. She started dating someone else, got married, and now has a beautiful kid. All that I hope is that she is happy because that's what she deserves. The same was said for Megan after we broke up. She later moved on and got married as well.

Now I did have another stint of happiness in my early 20's when I moved to Louisville, Kentucky to take an office supplies sales position. This stint was with Terri. I won't mention much about her because we were seriously crazy over each other. While our relationship was short and meaningless, it was more physical than anything else. We did have great times together, but she just loved attention from other guys. My family absolutely hated her because of the way she talked down to me. She was a former Miller Lite model, tall, long legs, huge knockers and a great smile. Again, far too hot to be with someone like me. To this day, I'm still not sure why I always felt this way. Maybe because I never really considered myself to be a good looking guy, although my old gray-headed Mamaw will tell you that I am the most handsome man in the world. That's what Mamaws are for right? Terri and I dated for a few months, only for our rocky relationship to end with me finding out she had been sleeping with my best friend/boss. This soon led to me losing my girlfriend and my job in the same day. As far as I know, she and my boss are still together to this day.

I still remember getting a text message from her a year later apologizing for the way she treated me during our relationship. I had already moved on so I didn't really think much of her apology. After swapping a few messages, she told me she had been diagnosed with Hodgkin's Lymphoma. For those who don't know, this is a rare form of cancer that used to be terminal, but now with the advances in medicine, the percentages of a cure and full recovery are pretty good. My heart stopped for a minute. Any time I had heard of someone having Hodgkin's, the result was never good. She told me she was apologizing to all the people she ever hurt, because she was scared God wouldn't let her into Heaven. I was absolutely shocked to hear this from Terri. I was so saddened to hear this news from her, and just replied with a message that she didn't need to apologize to me, and she wouldn't be making a trip up to Heaven for a long time. She thanked me for my encouraging words and I didn't hear from her again for another 6 months. The last message I received from her was that she had just been cleared cancer free and was ready to start a new life. I was glad to hear the news. With as much animosity you can hold against someone for what they've done to you, everyone deserves a another try, no matter what.

Now I tell about my relationships because each one has always led to the same result: me extremely happy and sad, then filled with drama, then unfaithful, and then losing the girl, usually because I've screwed up. The relationship ends. They find someone else. I end up alone, drinking, and listening to sad songs on YouTube, while at the same time all of my former significant others are cuddling up on the couch, watching a movie, with a glass of wine and a big smile on their faces. At least, after a bottle of vodka and listening to (insert whatever song makes you sad), it will make you think hard about yourself. This is where my life had gotten me so far. Several relationships all failed because my life was out of control. I don't know why I was like that, but it was my selfishness and immaturity that led me to always ending up being alone. I hated being alone. I always knew that I would end up finding someone else, at the same time; I didn't want to keep making mistakes like I had in the past. I got sick of living life that way when it came to relationships. I wanted to find someone that I could spend the rest of my life with. I had made every mistake possible when it came to relationships. However, I knew in order for me to mature and truly know what it took to be with someone, I'd have to make changes in my life so that I could be with someone. I feel like the only way I learned how to truly know what it takes to make it in a great relationship, was because I had failed so much. No matter how hurt I was during my relationships throughout my life, I could always count on Mom to be there for me and give me that motherly advice that moms always do. Mom had always been there for me, and had somehow managed to be the only woman in my life that never steered me wrong. Yet, for some reason, even she was about to be taken away from me forever.

"MOM'S NOT DOING TOO WELL . . . . AND THE DOCTORS AREN'T SURE WHAT'S WRONG . . . ."

In late June of 2009, Mom had woken up one morning and couldn't stop throwing up. She had been to the doctor recently only to find she had gallstones—due to have her gallbladder removed while her health was diminishing. With no other choice, Dad took Mom to the emergency room so tests could be done on her to figure out what was going on. After all, it could have been the gallstones that were causing her to throw up, but Dad didn't want to take any chances with her health at this point. With a number of standard procedure tests that are done in the ER, one of them involves checking the blood sugar level. Normal blood sugar levels range from 60-100. After Mom's first test, it came back at 1102. The doctor was so baffled at the results that he insisted on redoing the test, especially because if anyone has a blood sugar level that high, there's close to a 0 percent chance that they are alive. So, the 2nd test was done, and a different number came back, 1108.

At this time, the doctor pulled my father aside and told him she needed to be transferred to a better hospital immediately. Other tests were coming in showing that Mom was having heart strains, which could easily be confused as mini heart attacks or strokes. Her life was quickly taking a turn for the worse. The weather outside was so bad that they couldn't air lift her in a helicopter. Instead, they rushed her to the University of Tennessee hospital in an ambulance. UT hospital was less than an hour drive away. Time was very precious. None to waste.

From the minute of Dad taking Mom to the ER, and her being put in the ambulance, was about an hour time frame. During this time in our lives, my sister and her husband were living in Dallas. My brother and I were living in New Jersey, and none of us were prepared for the news. Clint and I were at a lake drinking some beers and enjoying a nice relaxing Saturday in the sun when we got the call from our brother in law, Steve.

"David, this is Steve, um, I'm not sure how to say this but I think you and Clint need to get home to your parents as soon as you can."

"What? What in the world is going on Steve?"

I was so scared after hearing the way Steve's voice sounded over the phone. It was as if someone had just died and he wasn't sure how to break the news.

"Something's wrong with your Mom, and apparently it's not good. [I could hear Steve take a deep breath, followed by a short pause] Lindsey just booked a flight to Knoxville, and I think you and Clint should do the same."

Steve explained to me what was going on with Mom since Lindsey was an emotional wreck and packing to fly home. Clint and I were too shocked by the news to even speak. We were more than a 10-hour drive from Knoxville, Tennessee. A flight out of Newark Airport was going to be over $1,000 a piece. Out of the question. Clint and I rushed to our house, showered, packed some clothes, and hit the road, completely nervous and scared about what was going on with Mom.

We ended up getting to Knoxville a little after midnight, and met up with Lindsey and Dad at a hotel to see what Mom's health condition was. All they could tell us was that Mom was on fluids and was in stable condition. We didn't talk much more than that since it was so late and we were all tired from traveling. That next morning, we all drove to the hospital and couldn't believe how disoriented Mom was. Unfortunately, when a patient's in the intensive care unit, only 2 visitors are allowed back at a time, every 4 hours. We went in shifts that would last 15 minutes, with Dad and Lindsey going first. Now, I have no clue what Mom talked about with them. I know it wasn't good. The 15 minutes we all got seemed to fly by much to fast. Clint and I patiently waited, wondering how Mom was doing. When Lindsey came back with Dad, you could tell just by her expression that Mom was in bad shape. I hadn't seen my sister cry too many times, yet it was obvious that she was wiping away tears as they came to tell us we could go back and see her.

I can't truly remember the conversation that Clint and I had with Mom, as she lay there with about 10 machines hooked up to her, but I do remember it being the toughest image of my life to see. She had no clue what was going on, or why she was even there. We tried explaining to her what had happened; she couldn't comprehend anything we were saying. Even worse, everything that came out of her mouth made absolutely no sense either. It was heartbreaking to see her like this. What made it worse was only getting to see her for 15 minutes apiece, every 4 hours.

While we waited in the hospital for the next 4 hours to pass, we sat in disbelief, worrying what she would be like the next time we saw her. In fact, we didn't even know if she would be alive. I don't know how many people out there that have been in a situation like this before, but I can honestly say that time never passes by any slower than when a loved one is barely hanging on to life, and all you can do is wait. About the only thing you can do is to remain positive, be strong, and know that the doctors and nurses are doing everything in their power to keep her alive. Thank goodness for the care that she was given while in the ICU because the more we got to see her, the better she appeared to be. Slowly, her blood sugar levels continued to drop down to normalcy and by the end of the week, she was released by the hospital. After a 7 day stint at the hospital, fighting for her life, Mom was diagnosed with diabetes and now had to completely live a different lifestyle than ever before. She could no longer go about her life drinking 10 cokes a day, eating pizza, or not exercising. She could no longer eat the traditional desserts we loved to have after a big meal, or even have a spoonful of ice cream that she dearly loved. Her life would now take a 180 degree turn from not only battling with her bipolar illness to monitoring her blood sugar levels for the rest of her life. It didn't really matter to us what changes would have to be made to her lifestyle; we were just happy to bring her home.

After getting her medication regulated and giving her a new pill to help her kidneys recover from the traumatic damage of her blood sugar being so high—Mom was back home. The new medication she was given was called Lisinopril. We didn't know much about it, but the doctors at UT were very confident in its ability to bring her kidneys back to normal. The first few days that Mom was home really took a team effort from Dad, Clint, Lindsey, and me to help her get used to a new routine. We all chipped in to help with Mom's first few days of being a diabetic. Everything from helping her prick her finger to produce a drop of blood, to getting the blood on a test strip for a sugar reading, and even to giving herself insulin shots. We were all there for her. We wouldn't have had it any other way. I was the only one that didn't give her a shot because for some reason my right hand wouldn't stay steady long enough for me to inject her medication. Dad usually was the one that helped with the shots. After helping her for the first weekend of being a newly diagnosed diabetic, Mom was back to normal. It was a very rough week for us watching Mom go through everything. The toughest part was seeing all those machines hooked up to her body, but Mom was a very strong person. We knew she would get through this, but mentally and emotionally it completely drained us all. Now that we knew Mom was going to be okay, we traveled back to our lives in Texas and New Jersey, confident that she and Dad were going to be just fine. Lindsey returned to her job at Six Flags in Dallas, Clint returned back to running a company plant in Kearny, New Jersey, and I was off to Philadelphia to start training for a new job. Things were finally normal for our family, for the first time in many years.

Just when things seemed to getting back on track for all of us, bad news awaited us right around the corner. In less than 2 weeks, life would take a complete turn for the worse, again. And again, it was Mom whose life would be in danger.

"AM I GONNA DIE?"

I couldn't stand to see Mom like that anymore. As that question slowly made its way out of her mouth, I had to leave the room. I had never in my life heard something as sad as that question coming from her. I quickly jogged out of the hospital and into the parking lot. As I covered my face with both hands, I burst into tears that didn't stop for nearly 5 minutes. Mom looked as if she just couldn't make it 1 more day in the condition she was in. I didn't think she would make it either. I mean just 2 weeks ago she battled through a blood sugar level that would've been the end of life for most people. However, this time, her blood sugar level wasn't the problem. Now she was dealing with something called lithium toxicity.

This had been the result of a dangerous combination of lithium mixed with her new medicine Lisinopril. She had only been on that medication for less than 2 weeks before it stopped her lithium from working. In fact, the Lisinporil made the lithium build up in her body to a level more than 3 times the amount that it should be because it wouldn't allow her kidneys to process and pass the lithium in and out of her body. She had become so bad that she was unable to speak or even comprehend what anyone was saying to her. For a "chronic lithium" patient, which is a patient that's been taking lithium for many years, the toxicity symptoms only start to show right when the person is close to dying.

Mom was in yet another life struggle, and once again, all of us came to her side for support. I unfortunately wasn't able to go back to the hospital for several days because I had just started a new job. I got a phone call from Dad early Monday morning, my first day at training, while I was in Philadelphia. Dad explained to me what was going on, and advised me not to come home because he didn't want me to see Mom in her current state. I tried explaining to Dad that it couldn't be any worse than the condition she was in several weeks ago, but Dad assured me that it was much worse. Also, he didn't want me throwing away this new job opportunity that I had just gotten. I couldn't stand being far away from Mom again while she was going through another health problem, but I could sense through Dad's voice that it probably wasn't a good idea to see her. Time just seemed to drag that entire day; all I could think about was Mom and if she was doing ok.

Later that Monday night, I did some research online regarding lithium toxicity, and to my surprise, there weren't many positive stories out there. I had even found articles that heavily advised against mixing lithium with Lisinopril due to the exact same reason that Mom was suffering from. Some medical research proved that it can be useful, but only when the patient is under extreme monitoring every day, sometimes even every hour by nurses or doctors. However, no doctor or nurse had told us that.

I called Mom's hospital room that night and I am still haunted to this day of our conversation. Mom couldn't say any word but "yes." I asked her several questions about what was going on, and if she knew where she was and all she could muster out was "yes." I couldn't believe my ears. Dad had warned me that she was in bad shape and to not call her hospital room, but this was my mother, and I wanted to hear her voice. I kept trying to convince myself that she was going to be okay. After talking to her Monday night, though, I wasn't so sure what would happen.

As word spread throughout our family about Mom's condition, everyone able to drive went to visit Mom, except for me. Even Lindsey had flown in again from Dallas because she was so worried about whether Mom was going to live or die. I kept getting updates from Dad and Lindsey for the next few days about what was happening. It wasn't until Thursday night that I got the news that this might be the end for Mom.

I was sitting alone in my hotel room trying to study for a test the following day, when I got a call from my Aunt Lynnette (my mother's younger sister) late that Thursday night. I stared at the phone and listened to it ring for about 15 seconds before I decided to answer. To be honest, I was too scared to hear what Aunt Lynnette was going to say. I knew that if she was calling me, and not Dad or Lindsey, that whatever news she was going to give me wasn't good.

"David, how are you doing?"

"Well Aunt Lynnette, I can't sleep, I can't think, and all I can do is worry about Mom, how is she?"

"Honey, I wasn't sure on whether or not to call you, but you have the right to know what's going on . . . ."

"Oh god Aunt Lynnette, ... what's wrong?"

My heart start pounding harder than it ever had, my head started hurting, my arms and legs went numb, my chest felt like it was going to explode. I felt like I was about to have a heart attack as I tried to hold myself together for what Aunt Lynnette was about to tell me.

"David, you might need to go ahead and drive down here as soon as you can. I've been with your Mom the last 2 days and things aren't getting any better. I'm not saying that, you know . . . .

Aunt Lynnette sobbed a few seconds. I could hear just by her struggling to find the words that Mom was in bad shape.

"Is she dying?"

"I'm not sure David, but you might want to come on down here. Now I didn't want to be the one to tell you what to do, that's not why I called. I just think you should know the truth about your Mom's condition, it's not good, honey."

Aunt Lynnette didn't have to say anything else because I knew I had to go back home again. Dad and Lindsey had been calling me every other hour for the past few days trying to assure me that Mom would be ok. Things had become worse that Thursday night.

I notified my trainers what was going on back home, and they were very sympathetic and told me to go on home. I was so tired and knew I wouldn't be able to stay awake during the drive, and I decided to go home the following morning.

It ended up being about a 12-hour drive from Philadelphia to Claiborne County Hospital in Tazewell, Tennessee. I got to the hospital just after 11 p.m. that night and ran into the hospital anxious to see what kind of shape Mom was in. Lindsey met me outside the hospital room, along with Aunt Lynnette, and they warned me about Mom's appearance before I went into the room. I'm glad they stopped me and said something because I wouldn't have been prepared to see Mom as bad as she was. I remembered how she looked several weeks prior when she was at UT hospital, but that didn't even compare to what her condition was now. Mom was asleep, unable to open her eyes to see me. Her body looked a bit swollen from the shock it had been going through, and her arms looked as fragile as I'd ever seen. I stayed as strong as I could in front of her and the family. However, the slightest bit of bad news or moaning from Mom would've had me bawling. As much as I couldn't stand to see her like this, I couldn't leave her either.

My brother had driven down a day earlier because he didn't want to be away from Mom either. He stayed with her the entire time she was at the hospital, and that's exactly what I wanted to do to. If she just got one last chance to open her eyes, I wanted to be there to tell her I loved her. No matter what, neither one of us was going to leave that hospital room. Clint and I decided to stay overnight with her in the hospital so that we could be by her side. Everyone left the hospital, while Clint and I sat in the most uncomfortable recliners trying to get some sleep.

I am not sure to this day if Clint slept at all. I didn't sleep for even 10 minutes. Mom moaned and groaned the entire night. She always made odd noises while she slept because she was dreaming. These noises were much different. They were so haunting and hurtful to sit and hear. I couldn't imagine how much pain she was enduring. Knowing how strong of a person Mom is; it had to have been hell for her.

That following morning, Saturday, Dad and Lindsey came into the room with Clint and me, and we waited together as a family just watching Mom. We looked for any type of movement from her eyes or body that would give us a sign of her condition. The longer we waited, the more concerned we became: she wasn't moving at all. The place Mom had been at for the past 6 days was a very small town hospital that didn't have much help to offer someone with lithium toxicity or any other serious emergency. Machines that were hooked into her did nothing but flush fluid through her system to try and get the lithium out of her body, since her kidneys weren't able to function. Many family members had pressured all of us to get her moved to Knoxville, Tennessee to a better hospital, but Mom's condition wasn't stable enough for her to be moved. Because her condition was so bad by Saturday morning, a doctor came to tell us that they had no choice but to move her to a better hospital where she could get better care. While the doctor wouldn't come out and say it, I could tell by the look on his face and his tone that Mom was dying. It was as if he couldn't even believe she had held on this long with all the terrible things that she'd gone through for the past 3 weeks. The doctor explained to us that Mom's condition was very unsteady at this point, and it wasn't worth the risk to keep her. He allowed us to ask him as many questions as we wanted, To this day I don't remember much of that part. I just recall that he didn't seem too positive or upbeat about her health. Within an hour of him telling us that he was going to call around to get her a room, we received good news that a hospital in Knoxville was going to make a room for her, Fort Sanders Hospital. After he left the room, Mom suddenly woke up. She was extremely disoriented and didn't have a clue where she was. We all gathered around her to let her know that everything was going to be ok, and that she was going to be transferred to a hospital in Knoxville. We kept trying to tell her what had happened. She couldn't understand anything that we were saying. All she knew was that she was in a load of pain and was in a hospital room instead of being at home in her bed. She reached up and scratched her eyes as the saddest question fluently spat out from her mouth without a hesitation, "Am I gonna die?"

I felt so sorry for what she was going through. I knew she was hurting so bad, and couldn't imagine what it felt like for her to think about her imminent death. (At this point I have to send a huge thank you to the doctors, nurses, and staff at Claiborne County Hospital and Fort Sanders Hospital, because if it weren't for your help, my Mom wouldn't be alive). Thank God that Mom didn't die. It ended up being several weeks of her getting the medical attention she needed to survive while at both hospitals. She made it though. I was so happy for her; so happy that she is still on this earth; so happy that she still has the biggest smile on her face when she sees me. Mom might be in her 50's, and me in my 20's, but I'm still her little baby. She'll always be one of the bravest and strongest people that I know.

Going through all this with her taught me that staying strong and remaining positive about the situation helps you handle it better. As long as you know, truly know, inside that things are going to be ok, then that's exactly what the outcome will usually be. It was the hardest thing to sit and see Mom battle for her life, but I knew she would make it. I never once questioned my optimism about her making it out of that hospital and getting better. To no surprise, that's exactly what she did. I'm so happy that Susan Chedester is my mama. I finally had my Mom back. I was happy with my new job (for a bit), and I was living with my brother for the first time since I was 13. Life was finally looking up for me and our family, with the exception of my "so-called" great job. It later turned out to be a disaster. It was like I was working and being managed by a bunch of 10 year olds. I ended up getting into the pharmaceutical sales industry, which is what I had wanted to do for several years. I had finally gotten the sales job that I'd always wanted. Things couldn't be better for me, or so I thought. Soon, life would be at its best for me. I finally met the girl that would completely sweep me off my feet.

DANIELLE

I had met Danielle at a restaurant in Dallas while I was down there for a training class for my new job in December of 2009. While my training was down in Dallas, the sales job would be up in New Jersey. Now, I have mentioned fate several times, although I still wasn't so sure that I believed in it, until I met Danielle. This *was* fate because Danielle was from New Jersey, and would be moving back there in May after her residency was up. Danielle was a nurse anesthetist, currently finishing up her final residency at a hospital in Houston. She graduated from Mississippi State, where she was also a cheerleader for the men's basketball team. We had bumped into each other at a steakhouse in Dallas and just randomly started talking. We chatted for a few minutes while we waited for a table, and I never really thought much of it, but eventually we had rediscovered each other on MySpace in early February. I mean I was extremely attracted to Danielle when I first saw her, but I never thought that I would end up getting in touch with her ever again. I can't remember if she found me on MySpace or if I found her; it didn't matter. We chatted for hours that first night we reconnected, and even when I laid down that night to go to sleep, I couldn't get her out of my mind. I don't know what it was about this girl, but she had it all.

She was amazingly beautiful, had the greatest personality, and just the sweetest voice I had ever heard in my life. Every time we talked on the phone I felt like I was on cloud 9 and never wanted to hang up with her. We would chat for hours and hours over the phone every night before bed. It felt like we were falling in love each and every second we talked. This was crazy! We hadn't even really hung out but we were telling each other that we were in love. We would talk on the phone until 4 or 5 in the morning just because we wanted to hear each other's voice. This was it. I had finally found the girl I was supposed to spend the rest of my life with. Just reading text messages from her would completely make my day. I could've been having the worst day of my life, but a short text from her that would say something like "I can't stop thinking about you" would immediately just put the biggest smile on my face. I was on top of the world and knew that I would never make any of those stupid mistakes again to ruin this. I hated being in New Jersey, so far away from her. However, it was only going to be a few more months until she was done with school. She would be done with her residency in Houston in May, and was going to move to New Jersey to be with me. She even turned down a $140,000/year job at that hospital in Houston, so that she could move to New Jersey and we could move in together. It also helped that her family was in Jersey too. While it is probably one of the most miserable states to live in, as long as Danielle and I were going to be together, we didn't mind living there until we could find somewhere else to start our future together.

I know it sounds crazy that we got this close so quickly and that we were talking about having a future together, but our feelings were so strong. It's unexplainable how happy we were. We both knew if our feelings were this strong over the phone that it would only be 10 times greater in person. Our friends even told us we were crazy. For us though, it didn't matter. All we could think about was February 25th, the last Thursday in February.

I was going to be down in Dallas again, this time for two weeks, for another training class. Danielle had some vacation days left and was going to come up to Dallas and spend the weekend with me. We were SO excited talking about it over the phone. We spent the last few nights leading up until I flew down to Dallas talking about how crazy we were for each other and how great it was going to feel to finally just get to hold each other. There were a lot of things I had been excited about in my life, but nothing compared to the excitement we both shared about finally seeing each other. Unfortunately, we would never get to have that weekend together. I remember that Wednesday being in class and how I hadn't gotten a text or a phone call from her all day, which was very strange. We were crazy with text messages. I bet we sent each other 500 texts a day. Later on that night she called me to tell me that her best friend had been killed in a car accident. She had been in the emergency room all day and night hoping that her friend would pull through, but she didn't. Danielle was so sad. I had never heard her cry before or sound this upset. She begged me to just grab her as soon as we saw each other that next night and just hold her and never let go. She wanted to be in my arms so bad, and I felt the same. At this point it was past midnight, and I needed to go to sleep because I had to be at training class the next day. And we both knew that the sooner we went to sleep, the sooner we would wake up, the sooner class would be over with, and the sooner we would be together. I had never been so excited to see someone in my life. Before we hung up, we ended the call like we always did.

Me—"I love you sweetpea."

Danielle—"I love you too baby."

I always called Danielle my sweetpea. And I always made fun of her because she couldn't think of a nickname to call me—I got called the usual baby or sweetheart. It didn't matter to me though. She was going to be my sweetpea for the rest of our lives. All we wanted was to be with each other forever. It's so unfortunate that we didn't get that chance. I didn't know it at the time, but that night was the last time I ever got to tell my sweetpea that I loved her.

The following day, Thursday felt like the longest day of my life. It was another day of long training, and I went without getting a text message or phone call from her. Houston was about a 4 or 5 hour drive from Dallas, and I knew that Danielle was going to surprise me by leaving early that morning so she could be waiting in my hotel room when I got back from class. Seconds went by; minutes went by; hours went by. Still no text or phone call. I would take quick bathroom breaks every 30 minutes and send her a text message asking how far along she was, but she never once replied. This wasn't normal. At least I had found out the night before why she hadn't returned my text or called me. That next day, though, I kept staring at the clock as it slowly was getting closer and closer to the day being over, and was still waiting for my cell phone to vibrate. All I wanted was just a quick text or call telling me she'd made it to Dallas. I kept trying to convince myself that she was ignoring me on purpose so that it would actually be a surprise when I walked into room 208 at the Courtyard by Marriott. I pictured seeing her standing there, all dressed up for me, with the biggest smile on her face, ready to jump into my arms and never let go. I kept feeling my cell phone in my right pocket, not making one sound. I kept whispering to my phone, begging it to vibrate, begging for a text message or a phone call. Sadly, I would never get that text. I would never get that call, at least, not from Danielle. I received a text message around 3:45 from Danielle's roommate Heather telling me I needed to check my hotel voicemail and that's all that she could tell me.

I kept replying with the text message "Why"? However, Heather wouldn't tell me why. She just said I really needed to call the hotel and check my messages. Before I even got a chance to walk outside the classroom and call the hotel, the back door of our training classroom opened up. In walked our training manager, Doug Cook, with another one of our trainers Traci Brackett, both with sad looks on their face. Doug was holding a small post-it note in his hand; he gently touched my shoulder and asked I me to follow him out into the hallway. We all sat down outside the classroom, while Doug stared at the note and then looked back at me with an odd blank stare on his face. I could tell something was wrong. Doug and Traci were always very positive and happy people, but at this very moment, standing out in that lonely hallway, this didn't have the feeling of anything happy.

"David," Doug started, pausing for several seconds trying to get himself together, "I have some news for you. Was your girlfriend driving up here today to come visit you?"

"Yes, I replied, Danielle."

I could feel something terrible had happened. Doug was struggling to tell me what he knew, Traci sat there with a blank look on her face, and I didn't know what to expect.

"There's been an accident David."

Doug was trying his best to look me in the eyes, but he kept looking back at the note in his hand and glancing at Traci. I was starting to figure out that this was probably not a conversation he'd practiced or even had before. All the years he had spent in sales, training, and management; nothing really prepared him for this moment.

I was on the verge of crying, but wasn't sure what I would be crying about.

"Oh God, Doug, is she ok?" I don't even know why I asked that question because just judging by the looks on Doug and Traci's face, I knew she wasn't.

"David," he tried with another long pause, as if he didn't know how to answer me, "I have the name of the hospital that she is at and a phone number for you to call."

"Doug please, is my sweetpea okay?"

"David, we don't know, just call the hospital. If you need to get a flight down to Houston, just let us know and we will get you down there."

"A flight to Houston? Oh please no. Is it that serious? Please tell me something other than for me to call the hospital."

I remember the look on Traci's face as she watched Doug and me go back and forth during this conversation. She looked as if she knew something that I didn't. As if she knew that Danielle wasn't in good shape. However, she didn't know. She was just scared and concerned for me, and especially for Danielle. Traci, who is such an amazing person, would end up being the first person I spoke to after I found out the next morning what had happened to Danielle.

I called the hospital and kept getting the run around from every single person I spoke to. I kept getting transferred every 1 or 2 minutes to a different department trying to figure out where Danielle was. Since I wasn't a part of her immediately family, the hospital could not release any information to me. I figured this would be the case, so I kept sending messages to Heather to keep me updated on what was going on. I mean, I still didn't even know what had happened, but just that she had been in a car accident, somewhere in Houston, and that's it. I didn't know if it was serious, or if they just took her to the hospital for precautionary reasons. At this point, I started doing what most people in this situation would do: I feared the worst had happened. I kept imagining different horrific things that had happened to her, and had almost convinced myself that this might be the end. I was hysterical and fell to the ground, squeezing tightly to my cell phone praying that I'd get a call from someone explaining everything that was going on. I stayed there, motionless, with tears slowly streaming down my face. I couldn't think of anything worse. My girlfriend, who I was deeply in love with, was hurt. I was 5 hours away from her and there was nothing that I could do. All I could do was hope that Heather would do her best to stay in touch with me.

Thankfully, I ended up getting updates. Class ended with me still lying outside on the pavement texting Heather, which meant I could finally leave and get to the hotel and have some privacy. My good friend at the time, Thomas Tocagna, drove me back to the hotel and kept asking if everything was okay, but I didn't even know how to respond. I just told him what I knew; that Danielle was involved in a wreck and was at a hospital in Houston. He urged me to get down there, but Heather had already told me not to come down. She knew something was very wrong and wouldn't fully tell me the truth. I went back to my hotel room in Dallas, anxiously waiting to find out what was going to happen. Even during the worst of times, I've always been so positive and optimistic about any situation that happens. As much as I kept thinking something awful had happened, I knew that Danielle would somehow make it through this. Just knowing how strong of a person Danielle was, I just kept thinking that this probably wasn't anything serious.

I wish that could've been the case.

I must've spoken to a handful of people over the phone for the next hour or so explaining what had happened, and just asked everyone to pray for her and her parents. It's strange how when things seem to take a turn for the worst, that my optimism seems to be at its highest. I knew that as long as I stayed positive and strong for Danielle and her family, that she would make it through this. Unfortunately, all of that would soon come crashing down with a short text message from Heather.

When I read the note from Heather that night around 7 p.m., I knew I would never see Danielle again.

Heather's text read:

"David, Danielle's car was hit on the driver's side this morning when she was leaving the neighborhood. The driver that hit her was drunk, going 70 mph in a 15 mph zone. He ran right through a stop sign and hit her straight on."

After reading that message, I immediately began crying. I couldn't believe this was happening. It wouldn't take a genius to understand that not even Superman could survive a car wreck like that. Danielle never breathed again after that wreck. She was airlifted to a hospital nearby in Houston, but her death was inevitable. Her parents in New Jersey wanted her flown to them to see her one last time. As much pain as I was going through, I had only known Danielle for short period of time. My god, can you imagine the pain that her parents were feeling? That's all I could think about. Were they going to blame me for this? For hours they tried to stabilize her so that she would be in a condition to be flown to her parents. While this occurred, I walked across the street to get some beer to calm my nerves. As much as I knew this was the wrong thing to do, I wanted the alcohol to help me escape everything. I wanted to run away from this problem and hope that it would just disappear.

Drinking always helped me run from problems for the last 8 years, but this would be the first time that it didn't help. Heather texted me with updates throughout the entire night, and as each text came across, I was getting drunker and drunker and crying harder and harder. I had several conversations over the phone with Heather, and also my manager at the time, Tom Lunsmann. I kept staying positive and saying that she was going to be ok. In the short time I had gotten to know her, Danielle was the strongest person in the world. She volunteered all the time for fundraisers raising money for cancer, dedicating her breaks during work to spend time with kids who were in the terminally ill cancer unit of the hospital. I mean, Danielle was the greatest girl in the world to me. Sweet, smart, absolutely beautiful, she would do anything possible to put a smile on someone's face. Even those poor kids dying of cancer loved it when she would go visit them. The last text I got from Heather was around 2 a.m. saying that she was being airlifted to New Jersey so her parents could see her, and then I passed out. In my head, just knowing that she was stable enough to be flown there, I thought to myself that she would be ok.

I woke up at 6:30 a.m. to my alarm going off and didn't have a text from Heather or even a missed call. Usually you hear people say, no new is good news, but not this time. I sent Heather a text message asking how Danielle was, and then jumped in the shower to get ready for training class. I showered as fast as I could, shaved, and before I even got a chance to start putting on clothes, I heard my phone go off. It was Heather. As I read just the first few words of the text message, I couldn't believe what I was reading. I looked away from my phone for a few seconds because I began to feel dizzy. The one message you never want to get, via text or phone, was what Heather had to send to me. As sad as I was to start reading it, I'm sure Heather was just as devastated to type it out and send to me. The worst had happened. Danielle was dead. I couldn't believe what my eyes were reading. She was really gone; forever. No more long talks on the phone telling each other how in love we were. No more getting text messages from her that made my day. No more getting to call her my sweetpea. All of that was gone, taken from me, taken from Heather and most of all, taken from her family. Can you imagine this happening to your child? Danielle was so young, bright, had a great future ahead of her; killed by a drunk driver at the age of 24. All because some idiot decided to get drunk all night and all morning and then get behind the wheel and drive. I sat on the edge of my bed, towel wrapped around my waste, completely unsure of what I was supposed to do. My girlfriend was dead, I'm 2,000 miles away from home, and all I could think about was that it was my fault. I wanted to crawl into a hole and never come out again. I didn't want to see anyone or talk to anyone. This had never happened to me before. It's similar to when I lost my Granny, but she was 73 and had cancer. Danielle was so young, and if it wasn't for me, she never would have been driving to Dallas that morning. I'd never be able to forgive myself for this.

I texted Traci Brackett and told her to come to my hotel room. Within 30 seconds there was a knock on the door. I opened it to find a look on Traci's face, the same look she had yesterday when she and Doug pulled me out of class. Just looking into her eyes I could tell how badly she didn't want to hear the news that I somehow uttered out of my mouth. My eyes were puffed up and filled with tears. My bottom lip and chin was shaking as I tried to muster up the courage to tell her what happened. It took me about 20 seconds to utter out the two words that still haunt me to this day. Traci was crying before I even got the words out of my mouth. I took one long deep breath, and barely mumbled, "Danielle's gone." I lost it completely. I started bawling my eyes out, harder than I ever had before. Traci grabbed me and hugged me harder then I had ever been held in my life. I soaked her left shoulder with tears. My-200 pound body had never felt so loose and dragging in my life. I told Traci I wanted to be alone and didn't want to go to class. She said she would inform the training manager and would stay at the hotel and make sure that I was ok. Within 15 minutes of Traci's and my painstaking conversation, my phone didn't stop ringing. I was getting phone calls from numbers I didn't even recognize. I didn't answer any of them. I just wanted to be left alone. So I turned my phone off and just cried my eyes out.

I pulled out my laptop and opened up YouTube so that I could truly mourn this terrible loss. I could barely see the screen when I was typing because my eyes were just pouring out with tears. I clicked on the search section tab at the top of the YouTube page. Slowly, I managed to type in our song (which will remain nameless) and listened to it over and over again. Tears just poured out of my eyes. I had never cried this hard in my life. The only thing that made this worse for me was that how many different things could have happened between the time Danielle got into her car and her to drive to Dallas. If only she needed to go to the bathroom before she left, put one more tablespoon of French vanilla creamer into her coffee, grab a bagel for the drive, anything at all that would have kept her from being at that intersection when she was hit. I couldn't help but to think, with everything that had just happened that this was my fault. If we never would have met, never would have become friends on MySpace, waited until Friday for her to come instead of Thursday, anything at all, maybe this would have never happened. And we could've had the time of our lives that weekend; possibly married now with kids of our own, with the white picket fence, and the family dog. But no.

And for many months ahead, I felt it was my fault. Even worse, I was told that her parents felt the exact same way. They wouldn't even let me come to the funeral. They didn't want to meet me; didn't want to even take a phone call from me. However, I couldn't blame them. If Danielle never would have even met me, their daughter would still to this day be alive. I was so depressed for so long after this happened. I ended up staying down in Dallas for the final week of training because I was friends with everyone there, and I knew it would help keep my mind off of everything.

My friend Tommy T. (Thomas Tacogna) who was on our New Jersey sales team, never let me feel like I was going to go through this alone. Still to this day I don't think he will ever know how much I appreciated him being there for me while we were in Dallas that next week and the following months afterward. He was the first person that I really talked to in person that Friday after I heard the news, besides the few minutes I spent with Traci that morning. He came and sat with me that Friday evening after class let out. I just didn't want to be alone that night. For the first time in my life, I was scared of what I might do to myself. The only thing I knew to do while I sat in my hotel room alone was to drink my sorrows away. He told me that a top executive of our company opened up that Friday class by telling everyone the news. He said several times during his telling everyone the heart breaking news that he got choked up and had to get himself together to let everyone know why I wasn't in class.

Tommy told me that some of the girls were in the bathroom minutes later crying and hugging each other as if they had lost someone of their own. All the people that were down there were the same people I was in training with that past December when I had first met Danielle. We were friends, and kept in touch with each other after training ended. I was deeply moved by the reaction that everyone else had after hearing the news about Danielle. As horrible as things were, I didn't want everyone feeling sad or being upset. I actually wanted to stay positive so that it wasn't bothersome or disruptive for everyone else.

I barely remember that weekend, but I do know that my friends never left me alone. They wanted to be with me just to make sure I was okay. I don't think any of them know how much that meant to me. There are still, to this day, pictures of me, Tommy T., and Natasha Prime (who was on the Philadelphia sales team and is still a dear friend of mine) posted on Facebook of us together that Friday night out at a bowling alley. I used alcohol to escape what I was going through that night, and many nights after that. This had become a common theme throughout my life. Anytime I was upset, I drank. Anytime I was depressed, I drank. Anytime I wasn't having fun, I drank. Anytime I was having fun, or wanted to have fun, I drank. No matter what I was going through in my life, I could use alcohol to control myself, or so I thought.

The next few months following Danielle's death are a complete blur to me. I spent every night drinking heavy amounts of vodka, mixed with red bull and a handful of tears. My life was at rock bottom and there was nothing in sight for it to get any better. I still remember one night at my brother's house, a few weeks after returning from Dallas, taking shot after shot of vodka just staring at the wall. My brother and his girlfriend were on their way to church, and before they were walking out the door, my brother turned to me and asked, "Man, we're going to church, would you like to go with us?"

A sarcastic chuckle came out of my mouth as I slowly turned my head towards him.

"Clint, why the hell would I want to go to church? I got news for you; there is no God. He doesn't exist. So while you two waste your time praying to some 'thing'" or person, I'm going to drink my vodka. But thanks for asking."

My brother had a sad look on his face. I mean, what could he say? I was completely out of control and there wasn't anything he could do about it. He was just trying to help me, but I didn't care. I was blinded by what had happened and didn't want help from anybody. Life wasn't being fair to me. Life isn't always fair. I understand that. But this had crossed the line; this should never have happened to Danielle, or her family. I knew one thing for sure: I didn't want to live anymore. This was the first time in my life that I didn't care if I was dead or alive. Somehow I knew if I kept drinking at the rate I was, I would end up killing myself. It's times like these where you never think anything will ever go right for you again. My life stayed that way for several months, until someone came along and finally put a smile on my face again.

EVERYTHING HAPPENS FOR A REASON

I remember sitting in my hotel room down in Boca, staring at what was before me: A bed that was nicer than I'd ever slept on in my entire life, a big flat screen TV that was sitting on a beautiful red oak stand, a mini bar/refrigerator that had everything from mini vodka bottles to M&M's, and a gorgeous computer desk, sitting adjacent to it a huge chair with a foot rest that was about the size of my couch back in Roanoke. For god's sake, the hallway to the bathroom and the clear glassed shower was nicer than anything that was in my apartment. My bags still sat next to the door, as I had barely unpacked anything.

Here I was, in a breathtakingly gorgeous and big hotel room at a resort people like me only dream about going to, but I couldn't help but to be sad. See, I had won this sales contest and trip months ago, while I was still dating Sheena. Winning the trip not only meant 3 free days/nights at this resort for yourself, but also included another person you wanted to bring along as well. Of course the only person I wanted to bring with me was Sheena. At this point in my life, she was just about the only great thing I had going for me. If we hadn't broken up a few months before, she would've been down there with me. I remember shortly after the bellhop put my bags in the room and left, I sat on the bed and cried. I felt lonely. Granted, it had been months since Sheena broke up with me and some of the things she said to me were completely unforgiveable, but I still couldn't get her out of my head. Now most people are depressed after a relationship has ended because they went from being extremely happy to being all alone. Most just miss the fact that they used to have someone there, and now that person isn't there anymore. This wasn't the case with Sheena. I really missed her. I missed everything about her and the things we used to do together. I wasn't sad because "a person" wasn't there to cuddle with me anymore, or watch movies with, or cook with. No, this wasn't the case. I truly missed her. I knew that "payback" would soon come for me after all the terrible experiences I'd had in relationships, I just wish fate hadn't made this ring true between Sheena and me.

I knew from the get-go that she was too good for me, but this time it wasn't because of her beauty. She was truly better than me in every aspect of our lives. She was far better looking than I was. She had a better personality then mine. She had a much better job than I did (she was a doctor). Her apartment was nicer than mine. Her car was far better than anything I had ever even driven before, much less ridden in. Really the only thing about me that could trump her was that I donated money to charities about once a month. That was about it. With all those differences between us, there was never a dull moment when we were together. I mean even when we cooked together every Tuesday night, we would spend most of the time laughing. I was floating over cloud 9 with this girl, looking down and smiling because the past 2 years of my life had been miserable and finally things were starting to look up.

It had been months since the death of Danielle when I met Sheena. I had spent most of my time just hanging out at home, drinking, and being alone. I didn't want to meet anybody, nor did I think I was ready to date someone else. I was still extremely heartbroken, and probably should've gone to counseling during that time, but I got through most of the depressing moments just fine. I mean, considering what I had been through my entire life, I was used to things always going wrong. That's why, when I met Sheena for the first time, I never thought in a million years that she would ever go out with someone like me. I didn't deserve someone like her. And even if we did date, I'm sure I would end up doing something stupid to ruin the relationship, just like I'd done in the past. While Sheena, to this day, will tell you that I didn't do anything to diminish our relationship, I still think that there were things I could've done differently, and that we would still be together. Sheena was Indian, with black hair like mine, and a darker toned skin color. She was a few inches shorter than I was, but just as athletic. I loved working out and exercising, just as much as Sheena did. After lifting weights and running for the past 14 years, I was getting tired of doing the same old workouts. So I ended up joining a kickboxing gym and fell in love with the workouts. I enjoyed it so much that I started kickboxing about 5 times a week. I was in as good shape as I had ever been (even better than when I played college baseball).

It was pouring rain one night when I stayed at Sheena's, and I didn't feel like driving to kickboxing class, so she insisted that I do Tae-Bo with her. I laughed thinking it was cute that she believed her little workout was going to compare to any workout I had been doing. I mean please, Sheena was in great shape and had a great body, but there was no way her workouts were even close to being as hard as mine. Boy was I wrong and I was dead wrong. About 15 minutes into the workout I was gassed! I was completely out of breath, sweating profusely, and by this time, not even doing all the exercises that was being called out. I glanced over at Sheena, only to catch her laughing at me, and she hadn't even broken a sweat yet. I didn't even finish the entire workout. I couldn't even walk normally because my legs were so sore. She made fun of me all night, but I didn't care. We both got our workouts in together, and this would just be another of many nights that I would stay with Sheena, and that's all that mattered to me.

I still remember the day when Sheena's nurses told me about asking her out. Her nurses really brought a lot of joy to me when I was in their office. They had come to this dinner event I had put on for many doctors and I spent most of the time at their table just talking and laughing. They asked me tons of questions, but whenever they asked if I was single, I remember looking down at the ground and almost bursting out in tears. I hadn't been asked this question since Danielle had passed away. I didn't even want to answer the question. It made me think how bad I wanted to go back in time and reverse what had happened to her. It wasn't fair, but life's rarely fair. As a result, I told them that I was single, which at age 26, isn't really something that I wanted to admit. Most people my age were already married, or at least engaged, with a family, kids, etc. I wanted that life so badly, but couldn't ever find someone that I wanted to settle down with. This was the life that Danielle and I would've lived together.

Anyway, the night went on, we all had a great time, and eventually it was over. I didn't think anything other than the dinner went very well, and tomorrow would be just another day. That didn't end up being the case. The following day I remember checking my company voicemail and there was a message from one of the nurses that had been at the dinner. She told me that I should call her as soon as possible because one of the doctors at their practice was single and interested in meeting me. I remember feeling like I was in middle school when I listened to this voicemail, because I was smiling and nervous, palms sweating, and I hadn't even met this girl yet! So I called the nurse back and she told me that I HAD to come in on Tuesday and ask Sheena out. I didn't really remember seeing her in that office when I was in there all the times before. I had noticed a very cute doctor in there once before, thinking that she was already married. I truly didn't remember this doctor. However, the way the nurses described her, I couldn't wait to meet her. When it came to asking girls out on a date, I usually wasn't very good. I got too nervous to do it and would find some other strange way to either get the girl's phone number or pass mine along to the girl on a business card.

I remember sitting outside of her office that Tuesday morning waiting for their office to open. I was so nervous that I called Tom Lunsmann, my manager, for a quick pep talk to pump me up and ask out Sheena. He just kept telling me that I sounded like a 5 year old when I told him how nervous I was. I remember him giving me some necessary advice, "Dude, stop being a loser and just ask her out." Wow, excellent counsel, Lunsmann. Thanks a lot for the pep talk. He laughed and told me to text him and let him know how things went.

I went into the office with my sales bag in hand, and my business card with my cell phone number written on it sitting in my shirt pocket. The nurses were there and all staring at me as I patiently waited for *her* to come into the office. As if it wasn't bad enough that I was nervous, Sheena wasn't even there yet. I had to wait around on her with all her nurses, and all of us knew what was about to take place. Well, we thought we knew. They all just assumed that I would smoothly make small chit-chat with Sheena, and then ask her out on a date, exchange phone numbers, and the rest would be history. This wouldn't even be close to what transpired. I watched Sheena walk in and go back to her office. My mouth was on the floor. I remembered the nurses explaining to me what she looked like, but when I first laid eyes on her, I couldn't believe how beautiful she was. I was nervous just based on the description they had given me over the phone. Now, in person, she was even better looking and I started just setting myself up to be denied. This girl wouldn't ever go for me. For crying out loud people called her doctor and paid money to come see her. Me, I got yelled at if I didn't bring cookies or doughnuts into an office for the staff! I couldn't do this.

There's no way this doctor was going to go on a date with me, based on the mere fact that she was a doctor and I was just some random pharmaceutical rep. The nurses, with their eyes staring at me, pushed me into Sheena's office. I don't recall much about what we talked about, especially because I was so nervous. I kept trying to figure out how I was going to ask her out, or at least give her my number. And, just like I figured would happen, we talked for about 15 minutes, she signed for the samples I had dropped off, and said it was nice to see me. I didn't ask her out or even give her my business card. I chickened out, as I knew I would.

The nurses tried talking me into waiting for her to get done with her patient, and try again. But that was too humiliating for me to do. Just as I had thought, I ended up giving my card to her nurse and ask that she pass it along to Sheena. I knew I would chicken out. It didn't matter because I wasn't expecting a phone call or even a text message from her. I got in my car, texted Tom that I chickened out, and went on about my day. I came home after work, went to kickboxing class, showered, changed, ate dinner, and sat on the couch to watch TV with my brother, sister, and her husband Steve.

Around 9:15, my cell phone went off; it was a text message. At first, I just thought it was one of my friends asking me what I was up to. Wrong. It was a text message from a number that wasn't stored in my cell phone as a contact. Could it be from Sheena? No way. Not after how I babied out of asking her out or even giving her my phone number. To my surprise, she wasn't as shallow as I make her seem. It was a text from her and I was so happy. I remember texting her that I was too nervous and intimidated to ask her out in front of all her nurses. After trading a few text messages, we agreed to meet for a drink the following day after work. I couldn't even sleep that night because I was so excited.

As I expected, that Wednesday took FOREVER to end. It seemed like the day strung along for 40 hours before 5:30 finally had come. Sheena and I met for drinks at this nice martini bar in New Brunswick, New Jersey. I couldn't get over how gorgeous she looked as I watched her walk towards me, while I stood in front of the bar waiting. Dad taught me that you always get there before the girl, because this was good manners and showed them what a true southern gentleman I was. While she apologized for being late, as I would find out through our relationship, she was always late (you know you were Sheena☺).

We had only planned to meet for a drink, hangout for about an hour, and then go on about our night. This didn't happen. I remember our talking and laughing for over an hour, while we sipped our martinis. Maybe it was fate, but we actually were forced to leave the martini bar because there was a private party at 7 that night. As we walked out of the bar, we both were having such a great time that neither of us was ready for the night to end. But Sheena was part of a volleyball team, and they had a game that night. We ended up saying good night and agreed to meet later on in the week for dinner. I remember driving home that night with the biggest smile on my face, so happy and excited about how good a time we had. I also remember wondering how Danielle would've felt about all this. Was she looking down at me upset that I was trying to move on with my life? For a few seconds, I started to cry, almost as if I was upset with myself for moving on so quickly. And then, I am not sure if it was her, but our song came on the radio as tears streamed down my face.

I still wasn't really convinced if there was a god or not because I hadn't been to church in over a decade. I hadn't prayed but once since I was 12 years old, and it was when I begged for Danielle's life. At this moment, there was no denying what was going on. It was as if God had let Danielle send a signal out to me, and it was a poignant moment. At just the very moment that I questioned moving on in my life with another girl, something like this happened. I cried as I sang every word to the song, just like I always did when it came on, but couldn't help but smile. The hair on my body was standing straight up, my body had the shivers, and I was truly caught up in the moment. Times like this still happen to me to this day, making me feel like Danielle is still watching over me. I love those feelings. Sometimes when I go run, the song will come on my iPod, and all of a sudden, during a nice day, when the earth is still and the wind hasn't blown once, a huge gust of wind will blow, and keep blowing during the song. All of these moments could be completely coincidental. I don't think so. It's at these times that I feel the most peace. I love it when those moments happen. Even after all the bad things I have done in my life, after all the times I've wondered if God has forgotten about me, or all the times I've wondered if there is a God at all, times like that occur. I can't help but to be thankful for those times. I can't help but to be thankful for even knowing Danielle and having her in my life, even though it was for a short period of time. And I couldn't help but to be thankful for the next 5 months of my life with Sheena. I knew that with this little signal from Danielle that it was going to be okay.

Although Sheena and I had just finished our first date, we were going to spend many more times together. I remember lying in bed with the biggest smile on my face. I felt a bit uncertain that what I was doing was ok or not. I continued thinking if I was being unfair to Sheena, myself, or even Danielle, by dating someone 4 months after Danielle's death. As much as I pondered about what to do, I managed to feel a bit of peace in my life. It was as if dating Sheena for a period of time was ok, not only with me, but with what I was going through. It had been months since I had a good night's rest, and that ended up being the best night's sleep I'd had in years.

And so, after several more dates, Sheena and I eventually started "officially" dating. Over the next few months, we became closer and closer as we usually spent at least 1 night a week together, including weekends. We did tons of stuff together that I hadn't ever done with another girlfriend before. We'd pick a Greek meal out of a cookbook and make it together once a week. We went out to nice dinners together. When it was nice outside, we'd throw the football around, which she was awesome at. We met at her apartment several times during the week for lunch and to just spend time together.

Now usually, spending this much time together with someone will drive me crazy. I mean, you have to have time apart from each other right? Not with Sheena. I wanted to be with her all the time. Even when we weren't together, I'd think of her. I mean, Sheena even watched Kentucky football games on the weekends with my brother and me. She'd wear one of the UK T-shirts I had bought for her and always come meet us out for the game. Even though I am sure that watching a Kentucky football game every Saturday wasn't at the top of her "to-do list", she still put on her happy face and had fun with us. We were so cute together I thought. She had the most beautiful smile that could just light up a room. We'd hold hands any chance we got and I loved that. The longer we dated, New Jersey didn't seem to be such a bad place after all. I mean Lunsmann even used to tell me that when I'd talk about her, my face would just glow. It made him sick, but I felt like a kid again. I couldn't believe that this was the same girl that I had been warned by tons of people not to date. See, Indians are typically raised to marry other Indians. Something to do with staying within their culture, marriages are arranged, and emotions aren't really shared between the two. I was warned by many other doctors not to date an Indian, because for her it would merely just be having fun for a while, and then, one day, it would be over.

I remember one of my favorite doctors. I swear we probably had more counseling sessions in her office than she saw patients. Every Wednesday I was in there talking with her about whatever it was going on in my life at the time. I recall her telling me a story about her dating an Indian when she was in residency. They had dated for 3 years, moved in together, and to her knowledge, were going to spend the rest of their lives with each other. Then, just when she thought the engagement was coming, he left. He told her that it was fun while it lasted, but he had to go find an Indian girl to marry so they could start a family. The longer Sheena and I were together, the more I sought out information about their culture. The more people I asked, the more my relationship with her remained in question. While we were having all this fun together, I was out defending her and our relationship to others. I kept telling people that Sheena was different.

She was better than having her parents arrange a marriage for her, or to just be in a relationship with me for fun. While we had a few times where things weren't 100% great between us, we still never had an argument or got mad at each other. We were so laid back that we just didn't see the point in being upset or arguing over something stupid. To me, our relationship was just fine. It was better than fine, it was amazing.

She had even mentioned several times about us taking a trip together. I'll never forget the day that she first mentioned us taking a trip to Europe together. Now, I'd only been out of the country once, and that was to play in a baseball tournament in Australia in 2000. Besides that, a vacation to Myrtle Beach, once to Orlando, and another to Atlanta to visit Clint in graduate school, I hadn't traveled much. Sheena loved to travel. She traveled all the time. She'd been to places I couldn't even imagine, and now she was asking me to go to Europe together? This was the first day I thought she was serious about me. Besides, who would go on a 9-day trip to Europe with someone they were "just having fun with"? One of her girlfriends was having a wedding reception in London, England, in September, and, instead of her just going to England for the weekend, she insisted we make a vacation out of it. I mean, we didn't even really have a big plan on where to go or what countries we were dying to see. When I say we never had an argument, I really mean it. When I mentioned that we perhaps visit Paris, Amsterdam, and London, she was completely up for it. Over a few weeks span, we bought our plane tickets, made hotel and travel arrangements, and the trip was booked! I was so excited.

We could barely sleep the night before leaving we were so excited. I was so happy to be doing this, especially with her. I figured our feelings were reciprocal and that this was taking our relationship to the next level. I know we had only been together for a few months, but we were always happy and had fun together, and to me, that's what relationships are about. Families getting along, respecting each other's jobs, enjoying the same TV shows—these were just things that came along with being in a relationship together. Those are things that don't always match up. They rarely will. We never really talked about those things. I remember Sheena mentioning that I should get my master's degree just so I would have one, but I never really thought it was because she didn't approve of my job. I mean being in pharmaceutical sales was a job I had tried for 3 years to get into. Finally, I had done it and was with a great company, had an awesome manager, and loved my job. Sheena was always a little uncertain about the pharmaceutical industry because both her parents worked for pharmaceutical companies, and her mother had recently been laid off. This was during a period of time where layoffs in the industry were happening all the time. And I do mean, ALL THE TIME.

As much as I tried to explain to Sheena that our company was small when compared to some of the "big players" in the pharmaceutical world, and that we'd never had a layoff, and that things were good, she still didn't seem to get it. Just to make her happy, I was going to get a master's in Pharmaceutical Management and Marketing from Drexel University. Not that I was just doing it to put a smile on her face, or to make her believe I did have a passion for furthering my education. It would've been a good thing to get a master's degree in, but she was adamant about me trying to pursue something else. I started to get the feeling that she was making me feel badly for only having a bachelor's degree in Exercise Physiology. I mean, I had made it through 4 years of college without even having a text book because I was so poor. Still, I managed to graduate with honors, and even taught Anatomy & Physiology Labs during my junior and senior years. I was a smart kid. Was I a doctor, no? Was I an engineer, no? Was I using my degree, no? But I had a great job, I did whatever I wanted, and was still able to help support both my parents. If they ever needed money to help pay hospital bills, pay the water bill, go to the dentist, or whatever, I was still financially able to support them. I know Sheena's intentions weren't to make me feel bad about my education or my job, but sometimes when she talked about those topics, it hurt my feelings. It almost made me feel inferior to her, much like how I started this chapter; how better she was than me. My job and education were just a few things she was a bit disgruntled about, and yet I hadn't even really told her much about my parents, or their health. I hadn't even told her about my parents' illnesses. Instead of telling her about them and about what it was like when I went home for the holidays, I just avoided that conversation all together. Besides, all that mattered was that we were happy and had fun, right? At least, that's what I thought.

Happy, excited, and anxious, we were off to Europe for 9 days together. We flew into London at night, and were so tired once we got there, that we walked down the block to a market, grabbed some food and wine, and just relaxed in the tiniest hotel room on the planet. Seriously, the room wasn't even 100 square feet! From what I had read, this was typical for Europe. Besides, we were only there to sleep, and the bed was quite comfy, especially with Sheena in my arms. We didn't have a schedule of things to do each day. We both had a few things that we wanted to see while we were in Europe, but just walking around and seeing the sights was good enough for us. Of course, the only thing we HAD to stay on top of was traveling to each city, because our tickets were booked months in advance. Sure enough, our first bit of traveling that following morning, a 3-hour train ride from London to Paris, we missed.

We had slept in, missed our alarm, and barely missed our train. We weren't too upset about it because we needed a little extra sleep, and we ended up catching a train 30 minutes later. When we got to Paris, I was amazed at how beautiful it was. I mean, I remember hearing other people talk about going there, and how much fun it was. I couldn't help but think to myself, as Sheena and I walked all over Paris, "Wow, here I am, a small town kid from Kentucky, now in Paris with a wonderful girlfriend." How much better could my life be? The museums there were unbelievable. Words can't even describe the architecture of the buildings and how discrete even the smallest things on the side of a building were sculpted. I still can't believe that I let Sheena talk me into climbing the stairs of the Eiffel Tower, especially because how scared I am of heights. While the tickets we bought only allowed us to climb up half of it, it was still high! You wouldn't imagine how beautiful the view of Paris is from the Eiffel Tower. It was so amazing. Besides the few times that the French were mean to us, we had a phenomenal time in Paris, but after 3 days there I was ready to travel on to Amsterdam. Again, just like Paris, the architecture was beautiful. But here, the people were much nicer and laid back. Of course, most of them were stoned, but they were still very nice to us. It was at a restaurant close to the Red Light District of Amsterdam that Sheena and I would have a conversation that completely changed our relationship.

I will spare most of the details. To no coincidence, it was storming like crazy as we sat outside underneath a huge umbrella that kept us from getting doused. Maybe this storm was going to be how our conversation was summed up, because I know Sheena felt differently about me after we got up to leave. I told her about my childhood. About how poor we were growing up, and about my fathers' struggle with Parkinson's Disease, alcohol and drug abuse, and mom's struggle with being bi-polar and having diabetes. I told her everything that she needed to know about me and my family that I hadn't already told her. I remember the look on her face as I told her about my "less than exciting" life that I had lived. I told her how that living through all the turmoil, it helped mold me into the strong, positive, optimistic man that sat before her.

However, it didn't matter what positivity I sputtered out about how we live and learn, and about how growing up without a lot of things, taught me to not be materialistic, and so on, and so on, and so on. Sheena still couldn't get past my parents' illnesses, and wondered if I had any of the problems that my parents had, whether it was with drugs, alcohol, or being mentally ill. Drugs were never too much of an issue with me because I had seen many of my friends become addicted to them and didn't want to fall into their lives. I did have periods where I experimented with marijuana and Vicodin, but nothing that went over the top or that would lead to an addiction. Hell, I was raised by a father that struggled with drug abuse. That wasn't a life I wanted to live. Alcohol, though, had been part of my life ever since I was in high school, and had become the one thing I relied on in recent years to help me get through life. Sheena and I both liked sharing drinks together, and this wasn't a big deal either, although I drank much more than she did.

While she never voiced a concern about how much I drank, I just assumed she was okay with it. However, the thought of being mentally ill or my possibly having a neurological disorder; that was what bothered her. Now, if someone was to observe me watching a Kentucky basketball game for 2 hours, they would probably feel that I acted bi-polar. That is usually the case for all UK fans. Not to poke fun at the illness by any means, or at my insane love for UK, that's not what I'm saying. However, I had witnessed mania outbreaks from my mother, and more so recently because she wasn't taking her medication.

I knew I wasn't bi-polar. However, I did have tremors in my right hand, never considering that I had Parkinson's. I was only 27 and knew I was far too young to have Parkinson's Disease. She even asked me if Clint, Lindsey, or I had ever gone to get tested for any of our parents' diseases. I lied to her and said I had been tested for Parkinson's, and I didn't have it. It still didn't matter to her. All this meant to her, especially because she was a doctor, was that I still had the possibility of being genetically "capable" of having Parkinson's or the bi-polar illness. She also knew that this meant our parents probably wouldn't be hanging out for backyard bar-b-que's or going out to dinners together. We had finally come to the realization that there were a few things that we didn't share the same view on. The family part of the relationship was very important to her, but in a different way.

It was important to her that our families spend a lot of time together. While for me, it was just important that she and her family accept my parents for who they were, and not judge them like so many other people did. The fact that she was a doctor was fine with me, but the fact that I was just a pharmaceutical rep wasn't entirely fine with her. While she had a degree that forced people to refer to her as "Dr." all I had was a 4-year Bachelor's of Science Degree, that didn't force people to call me anything other than David. Let's not even get started on the fact that I was a redneck from Eastern Kentucky, who was most likely expected to marry a white girl. While my parents didn't enforce that at all, it was one of those unspoken assumptions that most people have. My parents both knew Sheena was not white. In fact, from the first date we had, they both knew she was Indian. They didn't care. This wasn't the 1940s anymore. Race and ethnicity shouldn't be an issue, and they weren't with my parents or anyone else in my family for that matter. People's personal preference on who they want to be with is nobody else's business but their own. All that my parents cared about was if I was happy and was treating her like a lady. That was exactly how things were: I was finally happy again and always treated her right. Unfortunately, none of this mattered with Sheena's parents.

They didn't approve of us being together at all. Sheena still made me believe that her parents were "ok" with us dating. I knew that wasn't the case. I mean her mom still would talk to her about single boys that would be perfect for her to marry, because there were no medical problems in the family, and that he was a doctor, or engineer, or lawyer. I still couldn't believe my ears when Sheena told me, "If you told my father that you were in love with me, he wouldn't understand what that meant."

Are you kidding me? He was in his 60's and didn't know what love was. He didn't understand what love meant? How in the world can you be married to someone for over 30 years, raise 2 wonderful kids like her parents had done, but not know what love is? This was all part of those ethnic barriers that had differentiated Sheena and me. Even though she wasn't raised to really believe in the "fairy tale love story", I still figured she understood what love was, and that it could happen between us. Hope as I may, it never happened; with her it didn't anyway.

We enjoyed the rest of the time in Amsterdam and London together, and then flew back to New Jersey 5 days later. We were still getting along fine, and actually had another weekend getaway planned a few weeks later. This would be a camping trip up to Vermont, to spend in the outdoors with a lot of her friends. The trip was important and exciting for her, but I didn't share the same feelings. Besides, Kentucky was in the midst of a great football season, and when she broke the news to me that there would be no TV's there, I backed out of the trip. Instead of enjoying a great weekend with my girlfriend in the outdoors, I chose to watch Kentucky lose to Auburn with my brother in our tiny apartment outside of Princeton, New Jersey.

During those 2 weeks, post-Europe and pre-Vermont, I had turned down several opportunities to take a job promotion that would've moved me out of New Jersey. I was doing great with my job, even though I was contracted, and was having the time of my life with Sheena. However, she, my family, even my manager knew how bad I hated living in New Jersey. Even though my manager had a plan to get me promoted to South Jersey, where things were much more laid back and the people were not as mean, things just didn't work out that way. Every time my manager mentioned moving to Roanoke, Virginia, or Nashville, Tennessee, or Louisville, Kentucky, I would quickly shoot it down. I didn't even need to think about it. My life was great just the way it was. When I would tell Sheena about me turning down another promotion opportunity, though, she didn't approve. She had been taught to follow her career, wherever it may take her, not her heart. In her mind, I was an idiot for turning down these jobs. In my mind, I was doing the right thing because I was doing what I could to stay with Sheena.

This all came to a screeching halt one Monday afternoon.

Lunsmann was riding along with me on sales calls, and kept talking about this Roanoke position. I bet I turned him down over a dozen times over the past 3 weeks about moving down to Virginia. No matter what he told me about having a company car, getting a much bigger bonus, and being back in the south again and closer to my parents where I belonged, I still just laughed off his attempts. As I was dropping off Lunsmann for the day, Sheena was on her way back from Vermont. I had planned to go to kickboxing class, and then meet her at her apartment afterwards for dinner. Lunsmann tried one last time before he got out of my car to talk to me about Roanoke, but like all the other previous attempts, he failed. I told him I was starting to warm up to New Jersey, and that I didn't want to leave Sheena. As soon as he was out of my car, and I was on my way to kickboxing class, I immediately called Sheena. I couldn't wait to hear her voice, and was so excited to see her. As we talked, I could tell in her voice that something was wrong. I didn't know what it was, but she just didn't sound like herself.

Now, I had been in many relationships before, and I know that feeling of when the relationship is about to end it isn't very pleasant. I hated that feeling. As I drove on the New Jersey Turnpike, down to Old Bridge for class, I started to get that feeling. As I listened to her talk about the reasons why things just weren't working out, I started to think about all the conversations I had with my dad, with my brother and sister, about how I was the luckiest guy in the world to be with her. How happy she made me feel every time we were together. Sadly, this was coming to yet another end.

I didn't understand what had happened. We'd never fought or argued. I'd never cheated on her. She'd never cheated on me. We always had fun together. I mean for goodness sake we just got back from spending 9 days together in Europe! I kept thinking that maybe some of her friends convinced her while they were all together in Vermont, that she deserved someone better than me. How she deserved someone with a better job, of the same culture, that would not turn down a weekend getaway with her to watch a Kentucky football game. I still to this day think that conversation probably did come up, and that Sheena did think about how much better her life would be without me in it. How, if she just listened to her parents and ended up with another Indian doctor/lawyer/engineer whose parents weren't mentally ill, then her life and future would be better off. I didn't think Sheena thought like that, but maybe I was wrong. And on that Monday afternoon, I would be proved wrong.

Sheena was breaking up with me, but her reasons were something that I'd never heard before in my entire life. She would go on to explain that my job, my education, and my parents were constantly on her mind, but not in a good way. Some of the things she said to me on the phone were the most hateful words that had ever been spoken to me in my life. She, of all people, was making me feel bad because of my parents' illness. How, if we ever had kids, then I could possibly carry those genes and pass them along to our children. She even said, "I couldn't live with myself if we were married and had kids, knowing that you have the possibility of giving them a neurological disorder. I mean, David, I see how Muhammad Ali and Michael J. Fox are, and . . . . I just . . . . I don't think I could be with someone like that." I had never in my life hurt like I did when those words came out of her mouth. Losing my granny, watching Mom battle several times for her life, and losing Danielle were very tough things for me to go through. However, having someone that I deeply cared about talk to me like this was just heartbreaking. Instead of staying on the phone with her and trying to work things out, I yelled a few cuss words at her for hurting my feelings, and hung up. That would be the last conversation we would have as boyfriend and girlfriend. It was over. I had somehow managed to screw up another great thing that had been in my life. Just as I had thought before we first started dating, that she was too good for me, this had finally caught up to her and me. Truth is, she *was* too good for me. She did deserve better than me. But the person that she continues to search for isn't out there.

She was looking for perfection, the perfect guy. I know I'm not perfect, I'm not even close to even being in the same sentence as that word, but I do know that I have a lot to offer a girl. I offered as much as I could to Sheena; it wasn't good enough. I hated the feeling of not being good enough for someone. This feeling would haunt me for months, as I fell into deep depression yet again in my life. Not as bad as when Danielle died, although very close to it. As much as I had enjoyed every minute with Sheena, and thought we were going to be together forever, it was all gone. Even after the unforgiveable things she had said to me, I still had a very rough time dealing with the break up. Any other person would've sworn her off forever just based on some of the things she said about me and my family. I always was the guy that believed everyone should be forgiven, and have the opportunity for a second chance. This is exactly how I felt about Sheena. I tried so many times to get her back. It never worked.

In all honesty, I should've hated her for the way she made me feel and for the horrible things she said to me that day over the phone. And for a long time, I did hate her. But, I couldn't deny how happy I was when we spent time together. I knew that I could have this with someone else that would respect me for who I was, and not let my parents' illnesses characterize me as a person. It was time to move on. With Sheena being out of my life, I didn't have any other reason to be in New Jersey. I had hated the majority of the time I lived in New Jersey. It just wasn't the right place for me to be. Life was completely different up there then it was for me back in Kentucky. I wasn't meant to live up there anymore, so I ended up taking the job opportunity down in Roanoke, Virginia.

Up to the last day of me being in New Jersey, Sheena still treated me as if we were dating. As stupid as this sounds, to help me get over our break up, she agreed to continue acting as if we were still a couple until I left for Virginia. We still spent the night with each other, went on dates, cuddled, the whole nine yards. She did that for me, so I wouldn't hurt so much or be depressed. It really didn't work. Even though we still had fun together during that time, my heart was still broken. Even after those horrible words she said about me and my parents, I still couldn't get over her. We cried together several times before I left for Virginia. I tried to tell myself that when I left New Jersey forever, that I would never talk to her again. I wasn't strong enough for that either. She was anything and everything to me.

We texted a lot even after I left. We talked a few times on the phone and even spent a few days together when I was back in New Jersey for a wedding several months after I left. When I found out that I had Parkinson's, I knew I had to let Sheena know. I wasn't sure how she would react to it. In fact, to me, I was doing her a favor of sealing the deal on us never being together again, or at least that's how I felt. The last thing she wanted in a boyfriend was someone with an illness, especially Parkinson's. This was the feeling I had when I first found out that I had the disease. I remember asking myself, "Who's gonna want me now?" I knew that wasn't the right way to think. Any time my mind started to drift towards me feeling sorry for myself, I'd do whatever it took to ignore those urges and continue to remain positive. All I thought about was having people to be supportive of me. Even after listening to a doctor tell me about my disease, I kept thinking about how Sheena would feel, or even my father. Here I was, 27 years old, being diagnosed with Parkinson's Disease, and all I could think about was how others would feel. I didn't want anyone feeling sorry for me, or treating me differently. I wanted people to see how positive I was, and hopefully would inspire others to feel the same. I wanted to make other people see how much worse things could be in their lives. While I am not trying to make Parkinson's seem like no big thing, it's just that I've accepted that this is who I am.

Parkinson's is a very serious disease that many people struggle with their entire lives. In fact, the majority of Parkinson's patients never get over the clinical depression because of the humiliation factor that comes into play with their appearance. The way the world is today, being so materialistic, the main concern for most people is how they look. I was never one to think or feel that way, but it is impossible to run from being clinically depressed. You can only face it head on and either take medication for it, or do what I've done and just be positive. I felt that there were worse diseases that I could have been diagnosed with. It made me think of an old friend of mine I played peewee football with who had recently died from brain cancer; he was only 27 years old. To imagine the pain and struggle for life that he must have gone through during those times must have been unreal. There were so many things I wanted for OTHER people after being diagnosed that I never really thought of myself. Even Sheena, the girl who had broken my heart months earlier, was on my mind. Maybe this was me finally starting to grow up and mature. I had told her I couldn't have her as a friend when we first broke up. But now, after being diagnosed, I couldn't imagine having a life without her being my friend.

She had been my best friend over the past 8 months. I needed more people like her in my life, now more than ever. I cried so many times thinking about her not being in my life anymore. Many nights I spent alone, crying, feeling worthless. But now I had more important things to worry about. My life was now going to be completely different as a diagnosed Parkinson's patient. Now was the time that I needed Sheena more than ever. I needed outside support from my family and friends. I wondered how they were all going to feel once they found out, especially Sheena. I hoped she would still be my friend. After all, even though she completely broke my heart, I still wanted her to be in my life, one way or another. I just never imagined this disease would be the reason why.

I CAN'T HIDE IT ANYMORE

I still remember the first time that I told someone that I had been diagnosed with Parkinson's. It was at the end of January in 2011. While I hadn't actually heard a neurologist tell me I had Parkinson's at this point, I knew in my heart that I did. Within the past 6 months, leading up to early 2011, several internal medicine doctors told me I was in the early stages of Parkinson's. My tremors had become so noticeable, that there was absolutely no way that I could continue to hide them. I had learned several nifty ways to conceal these symptoms. Usually this meant always keeping my arms moving if I spoke, or keeping my hands in my pockets whenever I was walking.

I remember so many nights sitting alone in my apartment in downtown Roanoke that I would take a deep breath, close my eyes, lift up my right arm, take another deep breath, and then slowly open my eyes, hoping to see my hand being completely still. It never happened this way. No matter how many days in a row I did this, no matter what time it was, it wouldn't ever stop moving. I would do the same with my left arm, and it would shake even worse. The harder I concentrated on trying to make it stop only made the tremors worse. Whenever I would be at a restaurant, even the smallest thing like picking up my drink and raising it to my mouth would ALWAYS result in spilling it because of my hand shaking. When I had finally decided to come out and tell people about my health problems, it was difficult figuring out whom I would turn to.

The years of 2009 and 2010 were extremely strenuous for our family because of the up and down health problems my mother had.

My mother's bi-polar illness had become so nightmarish that telling her about me would not help. The last person in the world that I wanted to tell was my father, fearing that he would feel responsible for passing it to me. My sister was pregnant, and telling her would possibly cause more stress for her. That wasn't an option. My brother was extremely busy working up in New Jersey and had recently had his heart broken, and I didn't want to burden him with the news. For my immediate family, there wasn't anyone I could talk to. That really didn't upset me though. I had just moved down to Roanoke from northern New Jersey for the job promotion that I continuously turned down, and I was all alone. It wasn't the worst thing in the world. I was glad that I moved back down south. This was great because now I was closer to my parents, and even better, my Aunt Lynnette and Uncle Mark lived in Lynchburg, Virginia, which was only 50 miles away from Roanoke.

Aunt Lynnette was my Mom's younger sister, and I always had a good relationship with her. I remember when I was a little kid, she used to hold me down and blow what I call "stomach farts" on my little belly. I swear it used to make me laugh so hard I wanted to pee my pants, and she got the biggest kick out of it. Of all the nieces and nephews, we could never say her name, Aunt Lynnette, whenever we were little. Somehow, we all could only manage to call her "Nae Nae", which to this day I still call her. I remember her being around through the first 5 or 6 years of my life. She was an amazingly brilliant woman, and without a doubt the most athletic in the family. Aunt Lynnette had the unfortunate pleasure of growing up in Harlan, Kentucky. Harlan County was one of the poorest counties in the entire country. Movies have even been made about Harlan, *Bloody Harlan* (which is what it's most well known for in the southern part of the USA) and *Harlan County U.S.A*. Harlan was mainly a coal mining town and most of the families living there were very poor. The education system had to have been the worst in the state, if not the world. It was the type of town where girls were married and started having kids at the ages of 13 and 14. Rarely did anyone ever actually make it out of that town with a high school diploma and leave for college. Aunt Lynnette however did exactly that.

She lived out the dream of millions and millions of boys and girls that grow up in Kentucky, going on to play college basketball at the University of Kentucky. She was doomed with knee injuries that plagued her throughout her career, but still played, and to this day, can still claim that she played on one of the greatest teams in UK women's basketball history when they made it to the Elite Eight in the NCAA Tournament, only to lose to Louisiana Tech. She eventually graduated, went on to Liberty University in Lynchburg, Virginia, and got her master's degree in Christian Counseling. Also included in her time spent out to Virginia was meeting her future husband Mark Shadoan.

Mark was an Irishman, average height, red hair with a full beard, quite smart, and had to have been a smooth talker. I say this because Aunt Lynnette was extremely picky on whom she dated. I mean, one time, when Aunt Lynnette was playing basketball at UK, she brought home her boyfriend at the time, a basketball player on the men's team. To any UK basketball fan, we all knew who he was. Going from him to Mark Shadoan had to speak volumes for Uncle Mark. While I have known him for 17 years now, besides his exquisite tastes for great beer and food, the only connection he had to being a diehard Kentucky basketball fan was that his father grew up in eastern Kentucky. Also, his cousins that lived there were diehard UK fans. This is pretty much a requirement of all us Kentuckians. This was especially true for Aunt Lynnette, even more so because that was her alma mater. We live, breathe, sleep, drink, eat, and dream about Kentucky basketball. It's bigger than life to us.

Anyone that knows me and is reading this part of the book right now, and has been around me while I'm watching a Kentucky basketball game can completely agree with me on this. Watching the games together with my brother and my dad could give anyone a heart attack because of how crazy we act. Screaming, yelling, clapping, and cussing every 10 seconds for a 2-hour basketball game is enough to give anyone a heart attack. Somehow, Uncle Mark tolerates this whenever I go to their house and UK is playing. He knows when UK is playing bad because I will usually start throwing a huge temper tantrum. That is followed by Uncle Mark saying he's glad he can't see very well. He has limited vision because of an eye disease he was born with, that has gotten worse over time.

Uncle Mark's mother was born with that same eye disease that left her blind before she reached her 50's. She hasn't gotten the opportunity to sit on her front porch and watch the sunrise in over 40 years, but never complains. She's now 90 and doing just fine. I still wonder if she ever sits and thinks of what it would be like to see; to see anything at all: the clear blue sky on a warm summer day with nothing but the sun glaring down, a plane taking off from the airport, or even a squirrel running through her front yard. Well, Uncle Mark was born with that same preexisting eye disease that would slowly and surely diminish his eye sight. He's now in his 50's and can see somewhat, but it makes me sad to think how good a man he is, and that one day, he may eventually will go blind unless there is a medical breakthrough to cure his condition. Most people would sit back and say, "What did I ever do to deserve this," but not Uncle Mark.

If anyone spent 10 seconds around him, they'd see how joyous and hilarious he is. Sometimes he will walk into the living room just to do this stupid little dance because he knows it makes me and Aunt Lynnette laugh our asses off. He, just like my Nae Nae, is a Christian counselor. There aren't two better people in the world (except for my Uncle Jacob, Aunt Lynette's brother) that were born to be Christian Counselors. While they aren't allowed to tell me anything about clients because of confidentiality, I can only imagine some of the stories they hear about, day in and day out, but still manage to be the funniest and coolest couple ever. I've spent numerous weekends over there since I moved to Roanoke, and the majority of that time is either laughing or standing in front of the refrigerator just staring with Uncle Mark looking for more food to eat.

I didn't have a care or worry in the world when I was over there. I was always at peace, and felt like I could tell them anything. When it came time to finally telling someone about my illness, the first people I thought of was my Nae Nae and Uncle Mark. Now I had already read both of Michael J. Fox's books by this point (I'm pretty sure I read them both in about 4 days). He waited nearly 7 years before he told most of his family and friends. I didn't want to do that. My symptoms, from age 18 to age 27, while being very slow, had finally come to the point where they couldn't be hidden, and I knew they weren't ever going away. Actually, I've come to accept that slowly it will only get worse, unless a scientific breakthrough happens soon, which I'm extremely confident will happen. I wanted to be open about my illness since I'm completely fine with it. I mean geez, listen to any one of Michael J. Fox's interviews and he alone makes you feel great inside and out when dealing with Parkinson's. I knew that if anyone would be ok with hearing the news, it would be them. They were the first two people I told.

I still remember the look on Aunt Lynnette's face when I held my right arm up in the air to show her my tremors. Her first reaction was the exact same one that I would get from several other people that I showed this to. It was amazing that all of them asked me the same question. "Are you doing that or is your hand really shaking like that on its own?" I kind of thought, well yes, it is my hand shaking, but it's just that I can't stop it from what it's doing. Aunt Lynnette's left hand went from her lap straight to her mouth. I could tell that her initial reaction of this news was going to be that of what I was expecting, very sad and very emotional. Instead of letting her express those emotions, I felt the urge to stop her from crying.

"Nae Nae," I responded, "it's ok. I am going to be fine. Just think, if this is the worst thing that I have, I am lucky. Just think of all those other people out there that are dying of cancer, or have M.S., or Lou Gehrig's. Just think how much worse they have it. No matter how bad I think things are, there are hundreds of thousands of other people that are experiencing FAR worse things than me. If Parkinson's is what I am going to have, then that's just fine with me. Now can we get Uncle Mark to hurry it up so we can go eat?"

I knew that as long as I could assure others that the illness was not going to define me as a person, or change me, then it would be easier for them to accept the news. Aunt Lynnette gave me a big hug and told me she would always be there for me if I needed anything. She was so sweet and really helped me through this whole process.

The three of us piled into my car and drove off to get lunch soon after I broke the news to Aunt Lynnette. We never could decide on which restaurant to go to, and we always ended up going to some buffet so that any type of food we wanted would be available to us. While Nae Nae helped Uncle Mark get his food at the buffet, I told her it was okay if she gave him the news too. I had loaded my plate with grilled chicken and corn, and rudely was already eating before either of them got to the table. If my blood sugar got a little low, and I was very hungry, then my shaking was bad, so I started eating to try and keep my shaking to a minimum. Nae Nae, with Uncle Mark holding onto her right arm, came over and sat down. They both had the saddest look on their faces. I saw Uncle Mark take a second to gather himself to say, "Your aunt just told me the news, and . . . I'm . . . so . . ."

I stopped him. You see, I didn't want anyone feeling sorry for me. I didn't want anyone to feel pity, or to feel bad, or to even think that my life was over. I was still going to be the same David that always loves making people laugh, bragging about my photographic memory, and almost having a heart attack during every Kentucky basketball game. I can control my attitude. I can control the way I feel. The only thing I couldn't control was just my tremors, for now. I could see it in Uncle Mark's face and by the way he was talking that he was extremely upset. I told him it was going to be ok, that I was fine with it, and all I wanted was his support. They both told me (Nae Nae for the second time) that if I ever and they meant EVER, needed anything then they would always be there for me. Now, after seeing and truly feeling their emotions during this, I wanted to cry. It felt great to know that people were going to be there for me and be supportive while I went through coping with Parkinson's. Nae Nae offered to come with me to my first neurology appointment, but I told her I preferred to go alone. And that was that.

The biggest weight of my life had been lifted from my shoulders. They both now knew. In my mind, it was now two fewer people I needed to have that conversation with. The conversations we had weeks later mainly were the same old conversations we always had. Kentucky basketball, or some new great beer or restaurant that Uncle Mark said I HAD to try, or my arguing with Aunt Lynnette on why I should be her favorite nephew/niece instead of my sister. With them, everything was back to normal. Cooking, watching movies, going out to dinner, and the only time we spoke about Parkinson's was if I had told them about donating more money to the Michael J. Fox Foundation for Parkinson's Research, or writing this book. They made it so easy for me. I love both of them so much, and they both mean the world to me. However, even after telling them about being diagnosed, I knew this wasn't the end of the line.

This was only the start.

I was about to go to our company's National Sales Meeting down in Florida, and knew that I was going to have this same talk about Parkinson's with several people. Two people in particular stood out to me, Tom Lunsmann, who had been my manager while I was working up in New Jersey and Thomas Tacogna (Tommy T.) who was a dear friend of mine on our sales team. For some reason, whenever I thought about telling Aunt Lynnette and Uncle Mark, I didn't cry or even tear up. I knew I had to be strong for them and show them how much stronger of a person this was going to make me be. When I told them, while there were a few times where I came close to choking up, I held myself together pretty well. However, I had mixed emotions when it came to telling Lunsmann and Tommy T. I'm not sure what it was, but I remember sitting and waiting to board my flight at the Roanoke Airport at 5 a.m. on the first Friday in February, 2011, and almost burst into tears. I knew that they would take it harder than Aunt Lynnette and Uncle Mark.

FEBRUARY 5, 2011
BOCA RATON, FLORIDA

I had just gotten back from spending the day at the beach with a bunch of my friends from work. A lot of us were down there because we had won a sales contest from the previous year. My symptoms were going in and out every day but starting to be more prevalent. Some days I wouldn't shake as bad as others, but that Friday, I had noticed my right hand shaking much more than usual, causing me to keep it stuck deep into my pants pocket. The last thing I wanted was all my friends to see it and ask me the awkward question of why it was shaking. Most of the time, I found it easy to hide my tremors. However, another type of symptom recently started showing up that was merely impossible for me to hide. I noticed that I had developed a slight stutter, almost a slur to my speech whenever I would speak faster than normal.

On that Friday night, while a bunch of us were drinking, it was starting to become noticeable. I am sure that none of my friends really noticed, especially since we were having cocktails, and I am certain that no one thought much of it, other than I had a bit of a buzz. So I didn't say anything. I knew I couldn't hide my symptoms anymore though.

That Saturday morning, I woke up, and knew that I would have to tell my friends. I knew I would have to tell my manager. Most of all, I knew I was going to have to tell Lunsmann. While all of us were down there at this beautiful resort having the time of our lives, I didn't want my slurred speech to get back to my new division manager in Virginia. I'm sure if that conversation would've been relayed back to her, it would have involved someone telling her I had way too much to drink and was slurring my words. Not exactly the great impression you want people getting of you while you're down on a company trip. And definitely not a phone call your manager wants to get either. Once we all got back from the beach, I went up to my room to shower up and attempt to get Lunsmann to meet me before I went out to dinner.

Tommy T. had made dinner arrangements for me, him, his sister, and his fiancée (now wife, Crystal) at 8 p.m. that night, and I wanted to tell Lunsmann before I told Tommy T. By the time I had gotten back to my hotel room, it was close to 6:00. Since no one talks on the phone anymore, everyone just texts, I shot Lunsmann a few text messages asking him to meet with me as soon as possible. I really knew that the last thing he or I wanted to do while we were down on vacation was to talk about something serious like this. But I had to tell him, and there is no good time to meet with someone about such news. After a few failed attempts at getting him to meet with me that night, I called his phone and told him it was extremely urgent that we talk. Since Lunsmann always puts anyone he cares about before himself, he agreed to stop what he was doing and meet up with me.

I still will never forget the time between getting off the elevator to meet him, and the actual minute that he and I were alone to talk. I must've walked into 10 people I was very good friends with in that short 30-yard walk from the lobby elevators to the opposite side of the hotel, where Lunsmann and I had agreed to meet. Former New Jersey teammates, former sales trainers, former trainees I had been in training class with before, not to mention the parents of one of my favorite teammates in the world, Heather Wilson: all of them stopped to talk to me.

I had broken the news to Heather the night before, right after meeting her parents, probably a couple of the nicest folks I have ever met. I still remember how nice they were to me after I hugged both of them that Monday morning before they left the hotel. When I had broken the news to Heather, I remember seeing her face in complete shock as the words, "I've been diagnosed with Parkinson's Disease," rolled off my tongue and away into the night air. Since we were at a company dinner event, and surrounded by a lot of co-workers, I had made Heather promise not to cry because I didn't want her to be upset, and I didn't want to bring any unwanted attention to ourselves either during that private conversation. While her eyes filled up with tears, I told a quick joke to break the emotional tension and after her asking a few questions about me and how I was doing, the conversation was over. I knew it wouldn't be like that with Lunsmann.

After finally getting past all the friends I had bumped into in the lobby, Tom and I shook hands. I was dressed in an Italian suede suit and tie, since I was having a nice dinner soon and Tom was dressed like he just finished a tennis match in the U.S. Open. We barely spoke as we walked outside the hotel to this large canopy area where we could sit and be away from everyone. I was very nervous. It was somewhat easy to tell my aunt and uncle because they were my family and I knew they wouldn't view me any differently after hearing the news. Telling Heather wasn't such a burden on me because of the great friendship she and I had developed over the past year. She was a sweet, spiritual girl and knew she would be someone who would pray for me, and for a cure, which she promised me she would do. For some reason, I wasn't nervous at all when breaking the news to them, but this was going to be different with Lunsmann.

He had been my manager for the past year, and he had also been more than that. He had been a sincere friend, a true leader, an enthusiast, a motivator, pretty much anything that you could ever ask for in a phenomenal manager. All those problems I went through with my Mom and Danielle in 2010, Tom was there to help me. As much as he wasn't a part of my family, I always thought of Tom like he was.

I actually cried for a few minutes in my hotel room before I met up with him because I knew this would be one of the most emotional conversations I would ever have. Besides telling my parents, or my brother and sister, Tom had become someone very close to me. As we sat outside, he and I joked for a minute or two like we always did. Never a dull moment when he was around. If he wasn't teaching me on how to become a better sales person, we were laughing so hard that we were both crying. That was just his personality; the perfect balance between leader, manager, and friend. As our laughter stopped, Tom finally got around to asking me what was wrong. I'm sure he thought something was going on medically with one of my parents again, being that both of them had been through a lot in the past year. My head stared down at the floor as I could feel my right hand in my pocket shaking furiously. I started to feel a bit overwhelmed with emotions, but I managed to keep calm while we spoke. I told Tom I had something to tell him that was going to shock him, and that he needed to be prepared for bad news. As that sentence came out of my mouth, a small tear from my right eye streamed down my cheek and fell off to the floor as quickly as it had came. Tom leaned forward in his chair, as if he was watching the most suspenseful movie and the shocking ending was about to happen.

"Oh man, what's wrong?" Tom asked.

Before I started to tell him the story, another tear streamed out of my left eye and hit the back of my left hand, knowing the next 10 or 15 minutes that I had been dreading for the past few days were about to happen.

"Tom, I was in an office about a month ago and was filling out a form for one of my doctor's to sign, and she noticed my hand shaking as I was writing. The doctor jokingly asked me if I had too much coffee that morning, and I just laughed, and said no, it always shakes. The doctor then looked back at me and asked me a few more questions; questions about my family's health history, my eating habits, my exercising habits, more importantly, if I had ever had a concussion or any trauma to my head."

As I continued to tell the story, I could see Tom's eyes getting bigger and more curious as to what news he was being led on to hear.

"Tom, the doctor put me through a number of motor skills test. Tests that involved performing the simplest tasks mainly that involved keeping my arms and hands still."

I stopped my story, looked at Tom, and pulled my right hand out of my pocket. I looked down at it, and took a deep breath. As I raised it, it was shaking more then I had ever seen it before.

There we were, down in beautiful Boca Raton, Florida, staying at one of the most beautiful resorts I had ever been at in my entire life, and Tom was having to sit and listen to bad news. We were supposed to be having one of the most relaxing and joyous times of our lives. Instead, there we sat, both staring at the exact same image. My right hand 3 feet in front of both our faces, shaking uncontrollably.

"Dude, tell me you're doing that."

"No Tom, I'm not. I haven't been able to stop it from shaking for almost 9 years now. After seeing several doctors, and going through some preliminary tests, I've been diagnosed with Parkinson's Disease."

At this point, the 2 tears that I talked about streaming down my face had turn more into 10 or 15. I didn't want to be this emotional in front of Tom, but with the news still being so fresh to me, it still shook me up a little bit. This wasn't like having the flu. Not like I'd have it for a week or so, take some medication, then be back to normal in no time.

Parkinson's was going to be with me forever.

After all the research I had done about it, I was in the first stages of (EOP) Early Onset of Parkinson's. This merely meant the symptoms weren't as obvious, but the illness would eventually begin taking over full control of one side of my body, and then slowly take over the other side. It was coming whether or not I wanted it to and there was nothing that could be done to stop it. Even worse, Parkinson's had begun to affect my speech. My father's speech has been slurred for years, but he is double my age.

I was only 27.

The expression on Tom's face looked like he had just seen a ghost. Almost as if he couldn't, or didn't want to believe what he was seeing.

"What? Tell me you're joking," asked Tom.

For the next few minutes, he continued to ask questions as we sat together. Asking me about what else the doctor told me, asking me if I was ok, asking if I had told anyone else. After hearing probably the last thing he wanted to hear in the world from me, it almost seemed as if Tom had been through this before. As if through all the years of his life, all his experiences, it was like he had been through these types of situations before. Although he hadn't, Tom had gone through some worse things than I ever had—which is all a part of my positive outlook on life. NO matter how bad you think you have it, someone else always has it worse. We talked about Michael J. Fox, Muhammad Ali, my father, the symptoms, what I had been going through, etc. I remember telling Tom that I considered myself very lucky to have Parkinson's be part of my life. If this was the worst thing that was going to be thrown at me, then I was going to accept it and use it to motivate me. After all, there are so many more people out there dealing with far more worse things then what I am going through, so I don't really have much room to complain. Getting Parkinson's was my chance at having another chance to be a different person, to be a better person; something I had struggled to be most of my life.

Tom applauded my toughness and told me how proud he was to hear me speak so positively, especially since I had just recently heard the news. He said as long as I let people know this wasn't going to affect me or my life, then that was inspiring.

I shed a few more tears out of happiness that Tom was being so supportive. Imagine that, one of the top managers in a huge company telling one of his sales reps that he was inspiring. I had never been told that before. I never heard someone in my entire life express to me that I was inspirational to them, or that I could be inspirational to others. Man this meant the world to me. For a moment, he made me feel like I was on a talk show being interviewed in front of an audience about my illness. That I was there to share stories about how horrible my life had been and that I saw Parkinson's as a chance to have a new life that would inspire people. Was this what I was destined to do? Unknown David Chedester, a kid from small town Kentucky, turning a negative situation into a positive, and doing his best to use it to become someone great and help others.

Tom and I spoke for about 45 minutes underneath that canopy, and I felt so much better after talking to him. We stood up, shook hands and hugged. Tom and I had never hugged before. In fact, we would probably make some joke and laugh about us ever hugging. I felt like I was *living* in that moment. I felt his sincerity and also his sorrow for my having to begin this journey at such a young age. We walked back into the hotel together, talking and laughing as if we had just been at a comedy club. Things were already back to normal.

As long as it had taken for that talk to finally happen between Tom and me, it quickly had passed. Tom now had been introduced into the small circle of people that knew about my illness. This circle would soon grow into a large number of people over the next couple of days. We both agreed that I would need to tell my new sales team, the New Jersey sales team, and most of all, Tommy T.

We wiped our teary eyes before we said goodbye, now that our emotional rollercoaster had finally come to a stop. He promised that he was always going to be there for me no matter what, just as Aunt Lynette and Uncle Mark did, and just as Heather did as well. This meant the world to me. If Tom only knew how important it was for me to have that talk with him, and how much I dreaded it at the same time because I was unsure of how the company I was working for would react to news like this. Either way, it didn't matter anymore. Our little therapy session was over, and now life would move on. Tom gave me great advice on how to break the news to others. He told me how to break the news to Tommy T. in a way that wouldn't be so shocking and emotional.

I never was a religious person. I never really told someone I was so thankful that I knew them or thankful that they were in my life. But, as I hugged Tom again, and started my walk back across the hotel lobby to meet Tommy T. and the others for dinner, I muttered 5 words underneath my breath that I knew would've caused an outbursts of tears from me had I said them to Tom.

I took about 5 steps, wiped my tears away, smiled, and said, "Thank God for Tom Lunsmann."

IT'S A DIFFERENT VIEW FROM MY EYES...

Fresh off of being diagnosed with Parkinson's, I thought there were two ways that I could have reacted: negative or positive. I've always felt that for most people, it's much easier to be the negative person and complain all the time, then it is to always maintain a positive outlook on life. This type of person, while many won't claim it, seems to be what most people are. It's easy to think of anything that has gone wrong in your life and let it depress you. For the longest time, I was this person. It's strange how Parkinson's completely changed that for me, and gave me a more upbeat outlook. For 9 years the potential of having this disease had haunted me. I spent many nights tossing and turning in bed wondering if things would just continue to get worse day after day. For the last few years of my life, I've tried to always remain positive, no matter what, despite all the tragic events that I've had to live through. Negativity is the most contagious thing in the world, and the more you're around it, and surround yourself with it, the more it encompasses you, and takes complete control.

I've known so many people that were like this. They just wanted to complain all the time, even over the smallest of things. I'm sure we have all had friends or have known people that fit this exact description I'm talking about. The more you sit and listen to it, the more negative you become. Then you start to find something to complain about, and quickly search for someone to spread your negativity to. The process just continues to go on and on, and unless everyone seeks out counseling, the cycle will always continue. Since I have spent most of my working life in sales, I've had the opportunity to experience this more often than most, just because of the fact that sales jobs are very stressful. At national sales meetings in my career, I've watched this toxic process occur, several times.

I recall one night in Atlanta that still makes me laugh to this day. Two prominent sales managers stood in front of me complaining about this new policy that our company had just put in to place. It might not have been the best policy to add to our sales process, but still it wasn't worth complaining about. However, one little change completely ruined the lives of these two managers, from what it seemed. They stood next to each other, holding their beers, and complained for about 15 minutes. Since they didn't realize I was standing behind them, I just stood there and continued to eavesdrop. I mean, you would have thought these guys just found out that they both had to take huge pay cuts, give up their company cars, start wearing neon green bow ties, and have their health insurance taken away. These two guys were just completely blowing things out of proportion. I couldn't believe that this one simple little change had sent these two managers overboard.

Since change usually makes people uncomfortable, these guys knew nothing more than to complain about it. Finally, once they had drained each other completely dry of negativity, they needed to recharge their batteries, and feed off of someone else. They clicked beer bottles, both took a drink, and walked over to a few other managers that were at the bar. I'm not even joking, within five seconds into making small talk, one of the managers I was originally listening to started in on talking about the new policy, and how pissed he was about it. While this manager continued to complain, the other 3 just sat and listened. After about 20 seconds of complaining, one of the "new" guys chimed in with his negativity about the policy as well.

I couldn't believe what I was seeing. How easy and quickly this negativity spread from one guy, to two, and now to four. On top of all this, these weren't just any sales managers; 3 of them were actually the top managers in our entire sales organization. It made me lose respect for them because even though I didn't really know them, all they'd done over the past 30 minutes was complain. I mean just watching and listening to these guys was wearing me down, physically and mentally. I couldn't live like that. In other words, it made me wonder if I'd ever done something like this before. Had I ever acted out this exact same scenario before, or something similar? And if so, was there someone watching me or listening to me do it? Nevertheless, after watching this happen, I knew then and there that I had to become a more positive person. Was it really that hard to always be positive? I mean, I know we all go through things in life that will have a negative effect on our lives, but how we respond is what makes us who we are.

I always hear about people going through horrible things in life, and how negative an impact it has on them. I don't mean to generalize, but it takes a very strong person to be able to accept the tough times and move on. I've witnessed many friends and family go through hard times, and it seemed to have an extreme impact on their future. Either they turn to drugs, or alcohol, or depression, or sometimes even worse. Then, they always make up excuses for why their life is so miserable. Even I went through times where I used alcohol to run away from life and escape my problems. Sooner or later, though, you have to smarten up and learn that you can't continue to live life that way. I lived in this way for almost 10 years before I realized I had to change. Unfortunately, most people aren't always capable of making that conscious change. Time and time again, people just complain, become negative and make excuses for why bad things are always happening to them.

Even while writing this book, something very horrible happened in the world: the tsunami that hit Japan, in March of 2011. I remember hearing about it all day long on the radio while I drove around making sales calls. While I hadn't seen the footage of it yet, it sounded like a horrific thing to have to experience. From what it sounded like, anyone close to where the tsunami hit was dead. Millions were without power, and even with the tsunami coming and going, they were still in danger because of the fear of a nuclear explosion happening. Unless you were in a cave that day, you remember hearing about it. Thousands of people lost their lives. Some of the videos that leaked out onto YouTube showed the most horrifying footage of that day. Just thinking about how big the waves were, nearly 50 meters high, is just absolutely disturbing. I felt so bad for what was going on. Yet, I maintained a smile on my face and kept working. Granted, what was going on in Japan was thousands of miles away from the United States, but still, it was terrible. I remember taking a phone call that afternoon from someone that will remain unnamed. I listened to this person yell, scream, complain, and almost lose their mind over something so petty and so small. It was one of the most embarrassing conversations I ever had because I couldn't believe this person was so upset, and how upset they were over a very minor thing. I remember these words coming out of my mouth, "Really, you're yelling about *this*. A tsunami hit Japan today, thousands are dead, millions more are still in trouble, and this is what you called me about?"

I wasn't trying to make light of the situation that was being talked about over the phone. I was merely making an attempt at letting this person know that there were much worse things than what they wanted to complain about. However, my words only made the matter worse. The person ended up getting madder, claiming I was trying to change the subject, or blow off what we were talking about. The conversation ended up lasting over an hour. Not by my choice, but because this person just wouldn't shut up. I remember after we hung up, how tired I was and how my great day had just completely turned upside down.

Was I really going to let this person ruin my mood? Even more, was I going to immediately call someone else and complain to them about the conversation I just had? Was I going to take this person's negativity, let it grow and feed off me, and then pass it on to someone else? While this would have been the easy thing to do, I didn't let it affect me.

I sat in my car for a few moments feeling very sorry for the person that I had just got off the phone with. I looked down at my right hand only to see it tremor faster than usual. Stress or worrying about something typically made my symptoms worse. During several times of that ridiculous conversation, I felt my body tremble, and my right elbow even moved a few times, which wasn't normal, or even a symptom I had experienced before. There were also times during the conversation where I couldn't even get my sentence started because I was becoming so upset. I knew this wasn't healthy for me, or the other person. I wanted to just get out of my car and scream. This is what our world has become.

Here, I had tried to let someone know that there were far worse things happening in the world than what we were talking about, and all this person could do was grow even madder and more upset. Instead of taking a step back, realizing that things could be far worse, finding a solution to our conversation in a positive way and moving on, this person turned to handling things unprofessionally and negatively. It is what most people do, so I can't say I was surprised. I mean I had just been diagnosed with Parkinson's, and this person knew it. I had shared my new positive outlook on life before, and thought that I might have had somewhat of an impact on changing an attitude as well. Boy was I wrong. I haven't known many people that were diagnosed with a disease like this at such a young age, but remaining positive all the time seemed to be more challenging than what I expected. However, the more experiences I went through like this one, it actually made it easier on me. I now had experienced what it was like to be on both sides of the telephone. On one side, a person is losing his or her mind, throwing a fit, draining energy, wasting life, complaining about nothing. On the other side, someone sits and listens. That person has 1 of 2 choices. Let emotions be negatively affected and allow this to ruin one's day. Or shake it off, try and bring some positivity to the conversation, and move on.

When I was younger, I would absolutely have let this ruin my day, left work early, gone home and drank, but not now. I knew better than to go and do that. If I did, then the other person wins, right? The only thing I could do was try and remain positive on the phone, and still have a smile on my face after we hung up. I can't control what everyone else is going to do, or how they are going to react; I can only control how I feel. This, I knew, was going to be my toughest challenge throughout life. I guess it would be easy for me to just sit back and feel sorry for myself. After all, my family had lots of problems going on, and had been going on for a long time now. My mother was having many problems with her bi-polar illness that had a horrible impact on our lives and hers. Dad was living through a nightmare at home with Mom, which resulted in his Parkinson's condition becoming worse, and also resulted in him having seizures. I had other family members that also were going through struggles that included: fibromyalgia, blindness, unemployment, schizophrenia, child abuse, emotional abuse, and depression to just name a few. Now, these are all horrible things to have to live through. At times, they flat out seem like the worst thing imaginable. But, at the end of the day, they aren't. They don't even come close to touching the worst things in life. I mean people are dying of cancer, AIDS, and car crashes, every single day. Soldiers in Iraq are dying so that we can live our simple lives here in America. Just imagine being the parent of a soldier that is over in Iraq. I couldn't possibly fathom for a second what that would feel like. My aunt and uncle could probably write books on how many sleepless nights they had while my cousin Richie was overseas.

My cousin was a Marine, and served several tours of duty for our country, and I loved him and respected him very much for doing that. I remember giving him money to help pay for health insurance for his family after his wife gave birth to their first child, and how great I felt being able to help them out. I mean, he fought for our country for years; this was the least I could do to show my appreciation. There are so many other things that are going on all around us that are far worse then what we're experiencing. For years, I always felt like life was out to get me. Like everything in my life was always going to be bad, and that I would spend most of it feeling sorry for myself and complaining. And, for most of my life, this is exactly what I did. But, now that I have experienced what the negative side of life is like, I know I don't ever want to go back. I know how shitty that way of life can be. I want to change that, especially because it seems like we live in such a negative world. The world is full of too many lazy and negative people; something's got to change. I want to spend the rest of my life doing what I can to change this. Even if it's just one or two people that I can help, then that's worth it to me. Yeah, I guess I sound pretty cliché and sappy. And I am sure that most of us, at one time or another, have been the positive person and the negative. Probably more so the negative. Life's too short to be the negative. A 27 year old Parkinson's patient shouldn't have to tell anyone that. So whatever it is that's keeping you down or making you feel bad, it will pass. Stand up straight, smile, and just know that everything's going to be okay. I've heard it time and time again. I've said it hundreds of times, and I will say it again. Although it sounds much more inspiring from Michael J. Fox's mouth, "Don't wish for a lighter load, wish for broader shoulders."

I can honestly admit that being diagnosed with Parkinson's was the biggest turning point in my life. I could've easily used that as an excuse for always feeling sorry for myself and staying pissed off like the rest of the world, or for believing that God was out to get me. For a short period of time, that's exactly what I did. I drank a gallon of vodka every other day, and usually took a couple of Valium every night just to keep from having anxiety attacks. I chased off several people that cared about me because my drinking became out of control. Day after day I would wake up and have no clue of what had happened the night before because I was drinking until I blacked out. Here I was, writing this book and trying to help inspire other people, but instead I was living the exact opposite life than what I was trying to be.

In fact, it wasn't until I began reaching out to other Parkinson's patients that I finally opened my eyes and started becoming the positive optimistic person that I wanted to be. As rare as this disease is, it's amazing how close-knit the Parkinson's community is. The majority of that is all thanks to the wonderful things that Michael J. Fox has done with his Foundation for Research. I mean, can you believe that he, along with his foundation, has raised over 50 million dollars for Parkinson's research? If there is anyone in this world that I ever would want to be like, or follow in the footsteps of, I can't think of anyone else it'd be than him.

It's easy to say that because of how much he's inspired me; it motivated me to change my life and write this book. He almost makes you feel proud to be a part of the Parkinson's community. I know that many people really struggle with having PD, but it has been the best thing that's happened to me. I've talked with others that are dealing with Parkinson's that have felt the same way. Some have used it as a way to pick back up on old hobbies that help offset their symptoms like ice skating, skiing, or even hiking (higher elevations tend to help become less symptomatic). I even spoke with one person that whittles. This is basically the same thing as carving, using a special set of knives. My father heard this from a PD patient several years back on a chat website for Parkinson's patients and my dad even picked up on the hobby. You wouldn't believe some of the things he has been able to carve out of wood. The carving he is most proud of is a piece of wood he managed to shape into a nice looking hand stick. The top was a small sized basketball, painted blue and white for Kentucky basketball. The middle part or shaft was completely smoothed down with "UK Basketball" down the front side. One the back, it read "Coach Calipari". He specially made this to give to University of Kentucky Men's Basketball Head Coach, John Calipari, at a book signing event. I was so proud of Dad for being able to make something like that. Oddly enough, Dad was able to present that to Coach Calipari at a book signing he did in our hometown of Middlesboro, Kentucky. He was even able to get a picture framed with Coach Cal holding the stick. If this doesn't tell you how passionate we are about UK basketball: the largest picture in Dad's house is of him and Coach Cal!

It's amazing how many others have used PD to turn their lives into something positive. Parkinson's has helped me see the "good" that's inside of me, and the "good" that's inside of others. Most people are quick to find the things that are wrong with them, or that make them a bad person; not me. I know that all of us are great people with good hearts. It's in all of us. I enjoy living every minute of every day because my disease taught me to treasure all the happy moments. I always live in the moment. I cherish every day because you never know when it's going to be taken from you.

I spent a lot of my life pushing people away; scared to let someone get close to me because I knew rejection was always going to be the end result. My last 2 relationships ended because of Parkinson's, so this really affected the way I chose to allow others into my life. But hey, those two girls just weren't meant for me and that's it. I can't say my feelings weren't extremely destroyed to hear the words "I can't be with someone that has a disease" from my girlfriend. It is an extremely tough situation. I realize that most people don't want to be with someone that has any disease, especially Parkinson's because of the effects it has on their appearance. It was always fun while it lasted, but I look at it that they weren't good enough to be with me. I do realize that it takes a special person to be with someone that has an illness or disease. For me, I was lucky enough to be raised by a mom that was bi-polar and a father that had Parkinson's Disease.

I believe that growing up with my parents and seeing how much they loved and cared for each other taught me to see what's on the inside of a person is most important. For some reason, we've become such a materialistic world that it's almost impossible for most people to look at life or other people that way. Really when it comes down to it, our character is all we have. It's what makes us who we are. A person's true character always comes out during the good times and the bad. I have lived through some very tough times throughout my life, and I was fortunate to learn from every one of them that things would always find a way to get better.

I could've chosen to go down a different path once I was diagnosed with Parkinson's. Drinking heavily and staying depressed all the time would have been the easy way out. Especially for someone that's only 27 years old, having to deal with Parkinson's is very difficult. However, I have looked at this as one of my few opportunities in life to really make a difference. I realize that I am a nobody. I'm not famous, not a celebrity, not a movie star, not a rock star. I'm not even the most popular guy at the small gym I workout at.

But I do have a voice.

I have an inspiration inside of me to help this become a better world to live in. How I feel about myself is one thing, but I want others to think and know that I am a great person. I love helping people.

Whether it's helping with problems in their lives or just how to look at things more positively, I love to help.

I've never cared about material things. It's never mattered to me what kind of car I drive or the brand name that was stitched on my clothing. Flat out, I haven't even cared about money. Sure, having a lot of money is great, but what you do with it is a completely different story. I don't have much money, but what little I do have, I try to use it to help others. I'm not going to be the guy that outbids someone at a charity auction for a $2,000 set of golf clubs that will go to help a cancer foundation. But I do like to give any little bit I can to help charities and foundations. Because I know that if we eventually want to find a cure for all these dreaded diseases in the world, the money will have to come from us.

Finding a cure for cancer, or ALS, or diabetes isn't something that doctors and scientists are going to find lying underneath a rock. People that suffer from muscular dystrophy aren't just going to wake up one morning and be cured because they started eating more protein. These people need our help.

I need your help.

Dad, who shakes so bad he can't even eat a bowl of cereal, needs your help.

Nobody knows what lies in the future, for them or anyone else. However, I know exactly what lies ahead in my future: giving. For as long as I live, I will never stop giving to help find a cure. Parkinson's and this book have given me my one opportunity to try and help. I am going to give the rest of my life and dedicate it to help raise awareness and money for Parkinson's research. For all that time I was part of a problem, it is now time for me to help find the solution. Parkinson's has given me the opportunity to take my time and devote it to helping others. I do know that Parkinson's will continue to take from me. It may someday take away my ability to kickbox or run or catch a football. It might one day even take away my ability to go for a light jog or even type on a computer. It even could take away my ability to hold my first child. But I do know one thing; it will never take away my character. It won't ever take away my inspiration, and it won't ever take away my heart.

CPSIA information can be obtained at www.ICGtesting.com
Printed in the USA
BVOW061900270312

286216BV00003B/2/P